FALL 2020

STYLE & DESIGN:

MODERN CABIN IN THE WOODS - PHOTO STORY BY MAXWELL ALEXANDER
P.2

WORKING FROM HOME WITH KEI KULLBERG
P.14

FARM HOUSE REINVENETED BY DUNCAN AVENUE DESIGN STUDIO
P.26

IN THE BUSINESS OF BEAUTY - INTERVIEW WITH DR. ZAINAB MOGUL-ASHRAF OF HEBE MEDICAL SPA
P.40

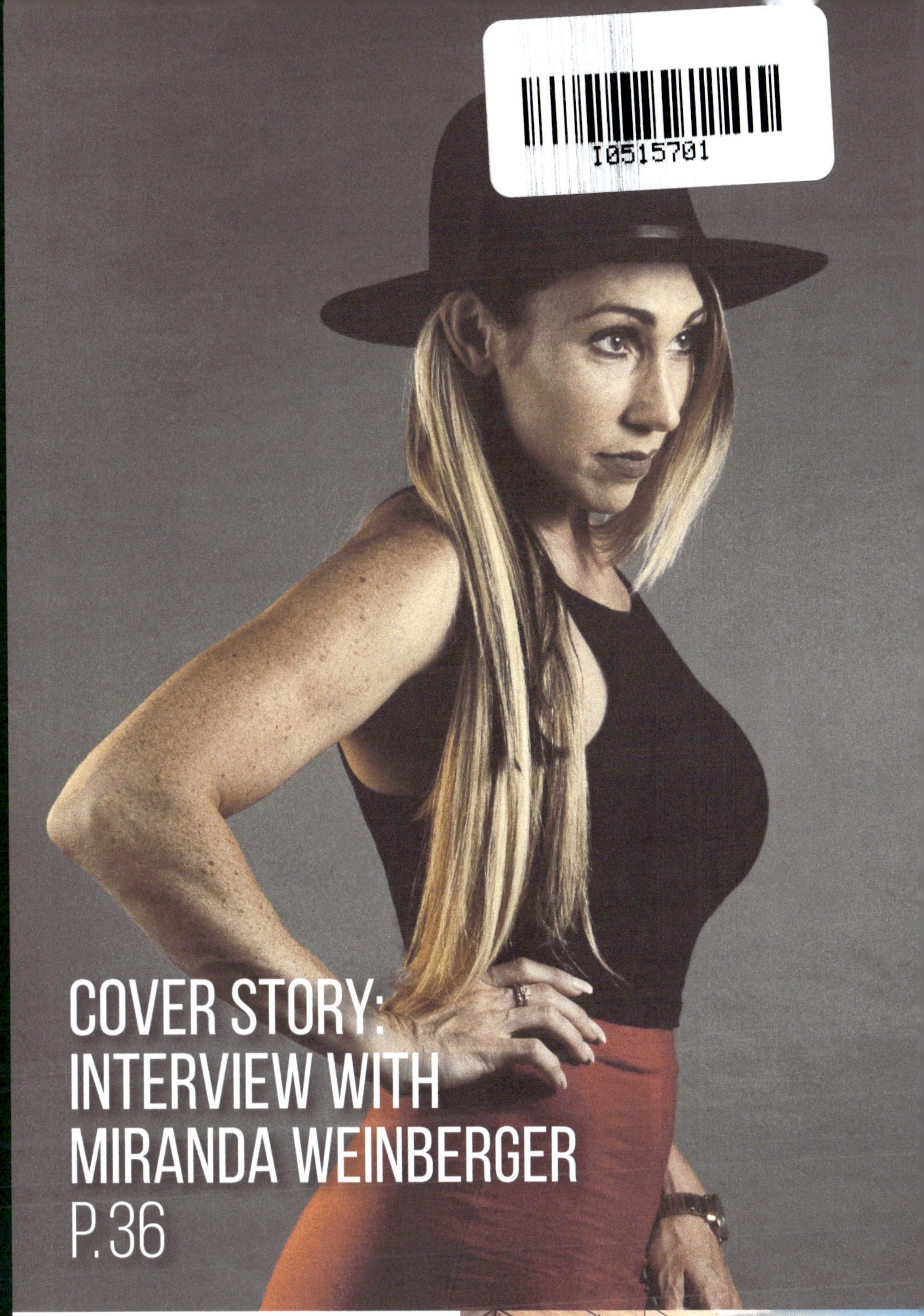

COVER STORY: INTERVIEW WITH MIRANDA WEINBERGER
P.36

| FROM THE EDITOR:

This fall (and the entire year) is like no other for so many reasons, but one thing will always be true: beauty will eventually save the world :)

In this issue, we are talking about internal and external beauty and showcasing brands, individuals, and design projects that bring more beauty into our lives.

All is and will be well!

Maxwell Alexander, Editor-in-chief

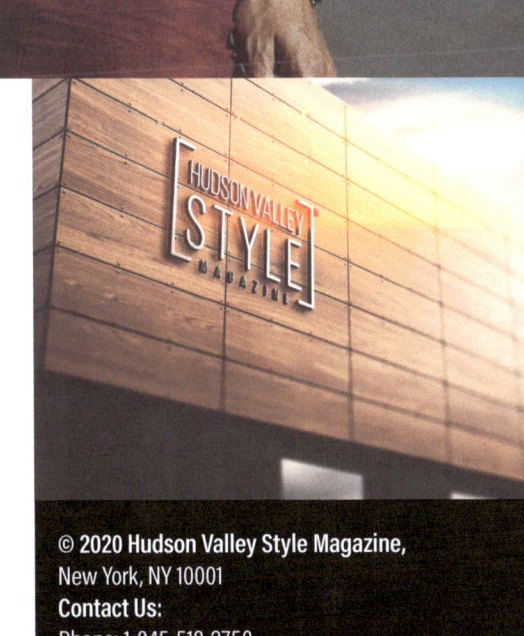

© 2020 Hudson Valley Style Magazine,
New York, NY 10001
Contact Us:
Phone: 1-845-518-2750
E-mail: hello@hudsonvalley.style

HUDSON VALLEY **STYLE** 1

FRESH AIR, INSPIRING DESIGN, WARMTH & COMFORT...
MAITOPIA PHOTO STORY BY MAXWELL ALEXANDER

Escape the craziness for a few days and keep a healthy distance from the rest of the World in Maitopia, Hudson Valley's hidden modern rustic gem in the middle of the woods in Red Hook, New York.

This beautifully designed passive glass & wood modern cabin offers elegant details and the warmth that only an upstate energy-efficient retreat could. With a soaking egg tub, fires at every turn and a year-round hot pool you will fall in love with the place and the towns nearby.

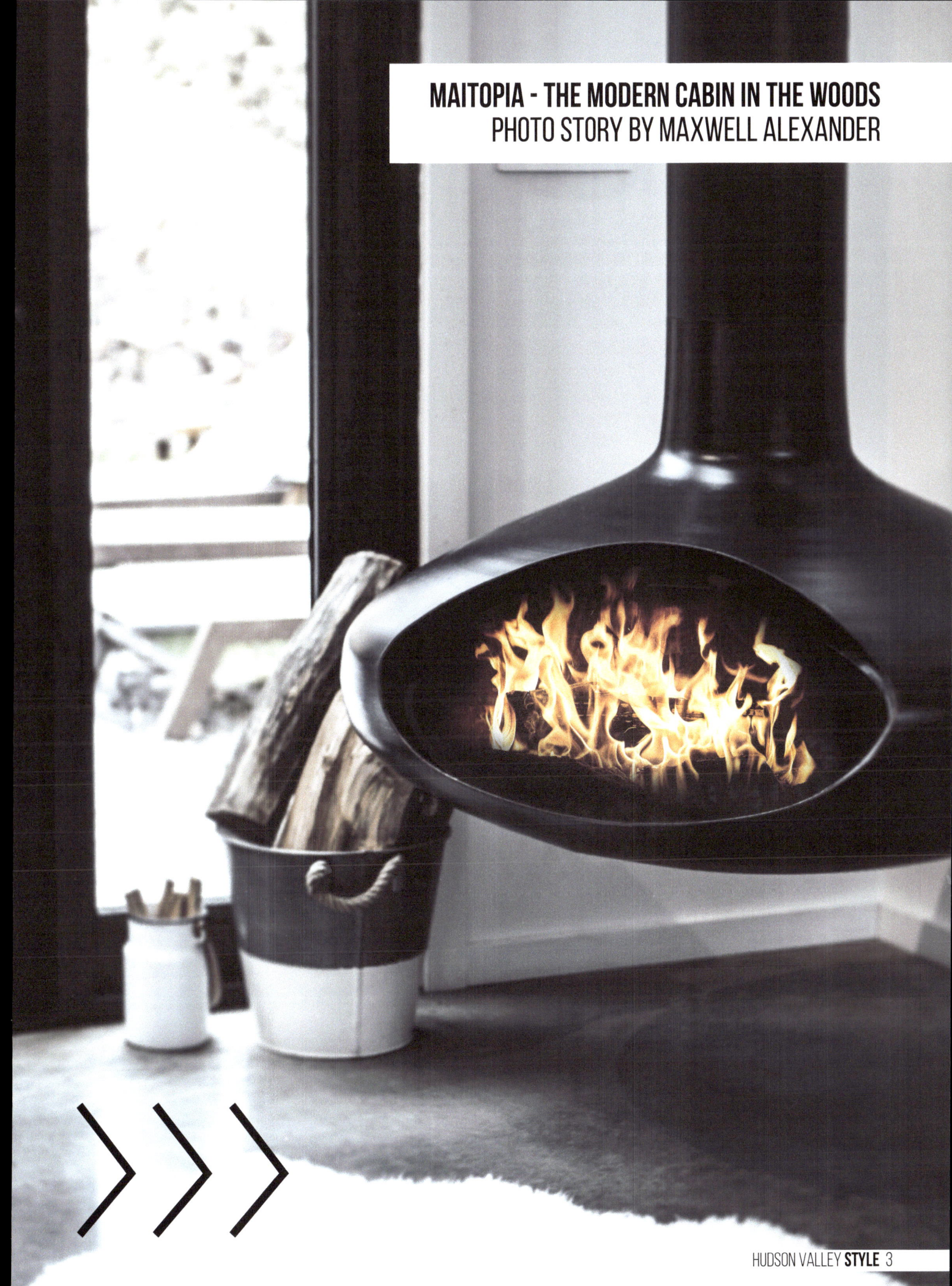

MAITOPIA - THE MODERN CABIN IN THE WOODS
PHOTO STORY BY MAXWELL ALEXANDER

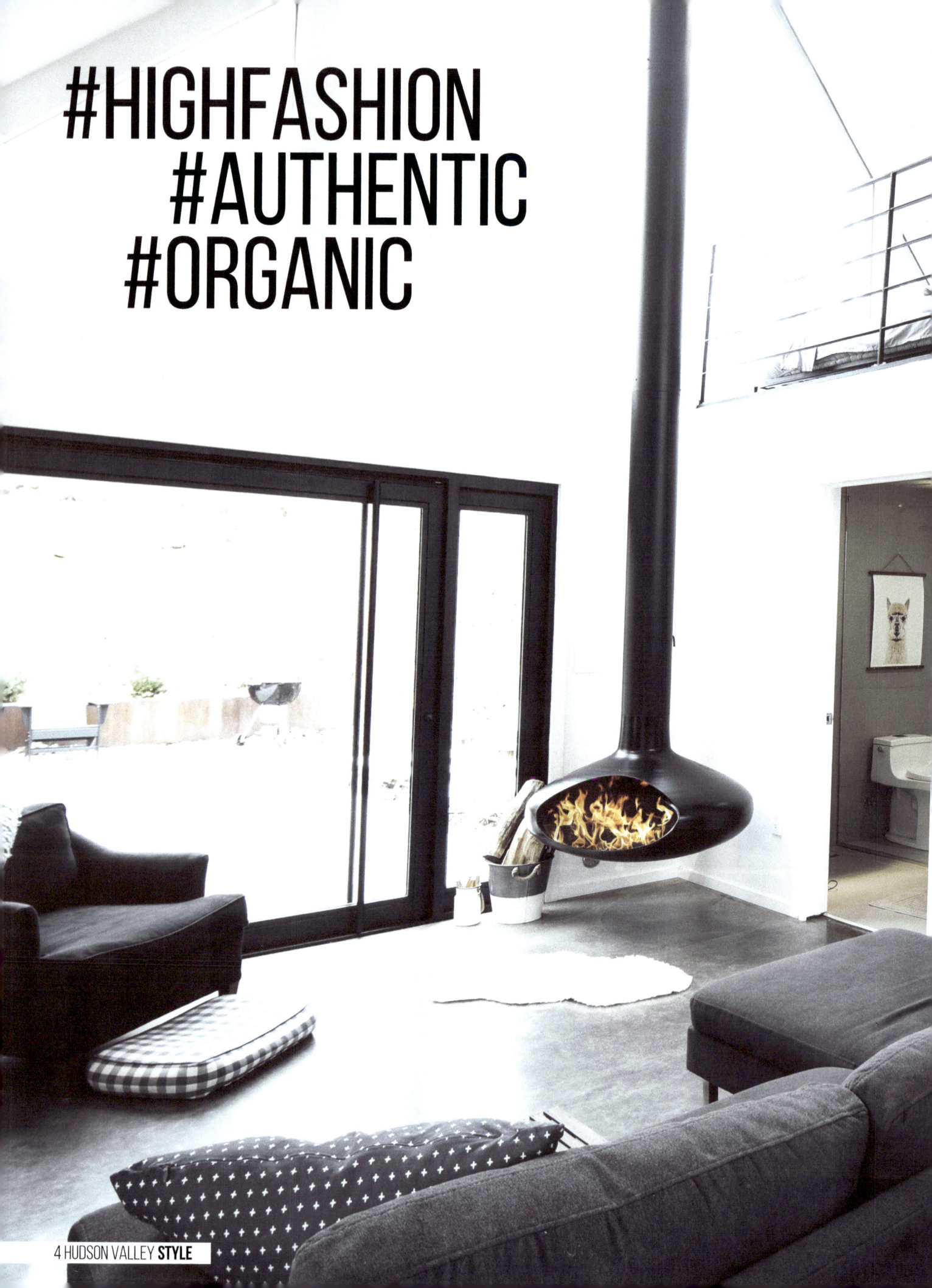

#HIGHFASHION #AUTHENTIC #ORGANIC

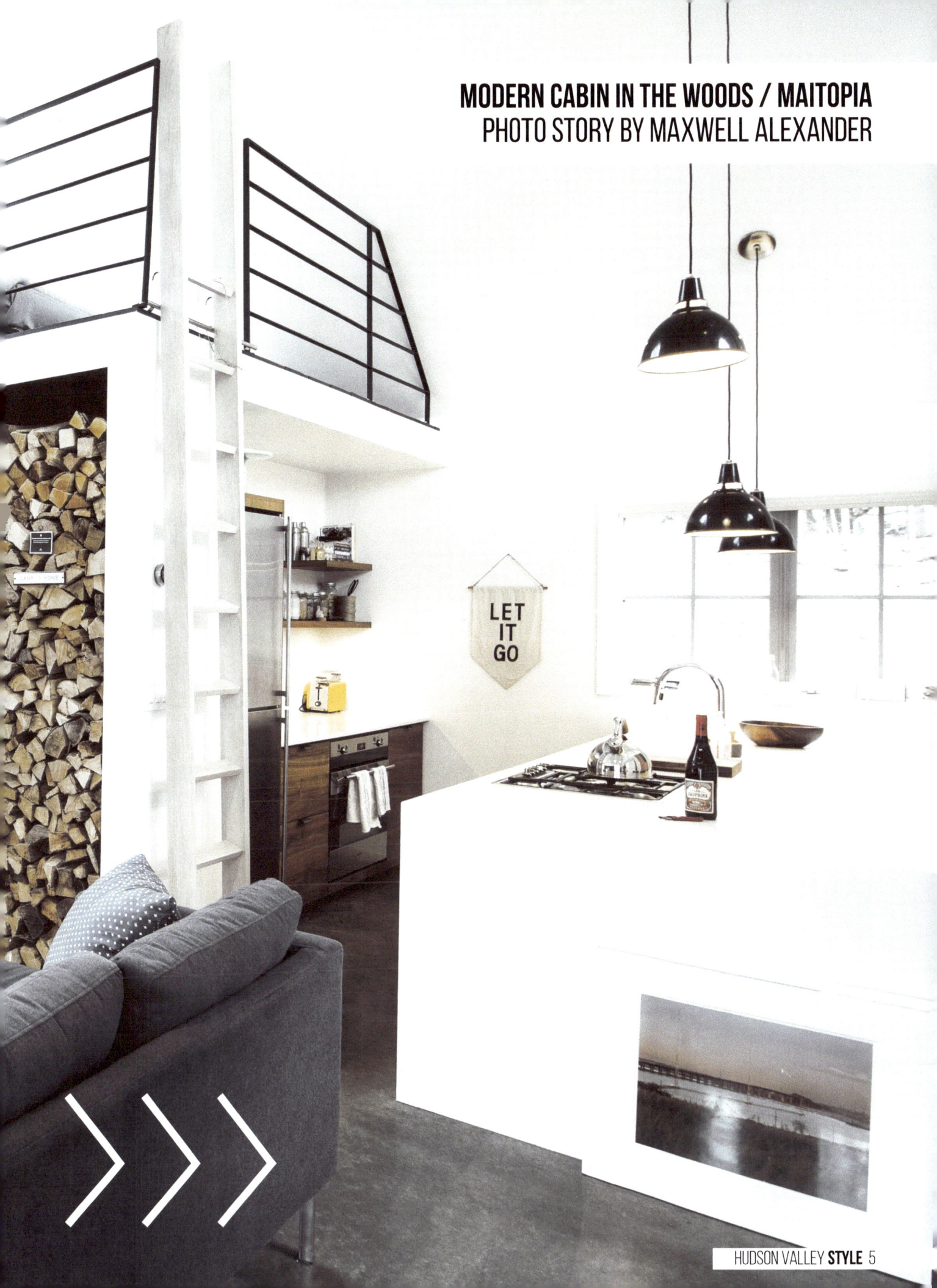

MODERN CABIN IN THE WOODS / MAITOPIA
PHOTO STORY BY MAXWELL ALEXANDER

#STYLE #DESIGN #HUDSONVALLEY

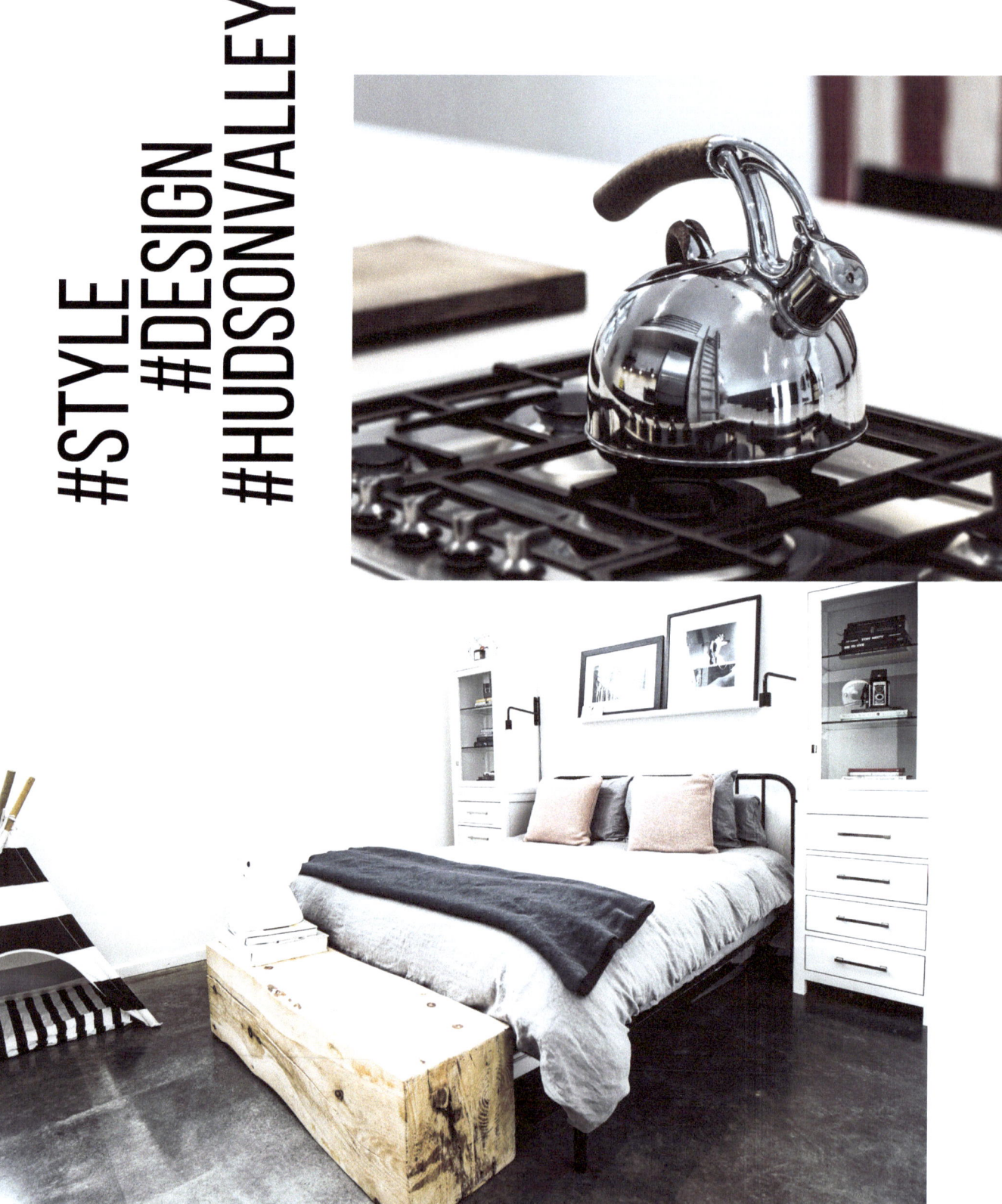

MODERN CABIN IN THE WOODS / MAITOPIA
PHOTO STORY BY MAXWELL ALEXANDER

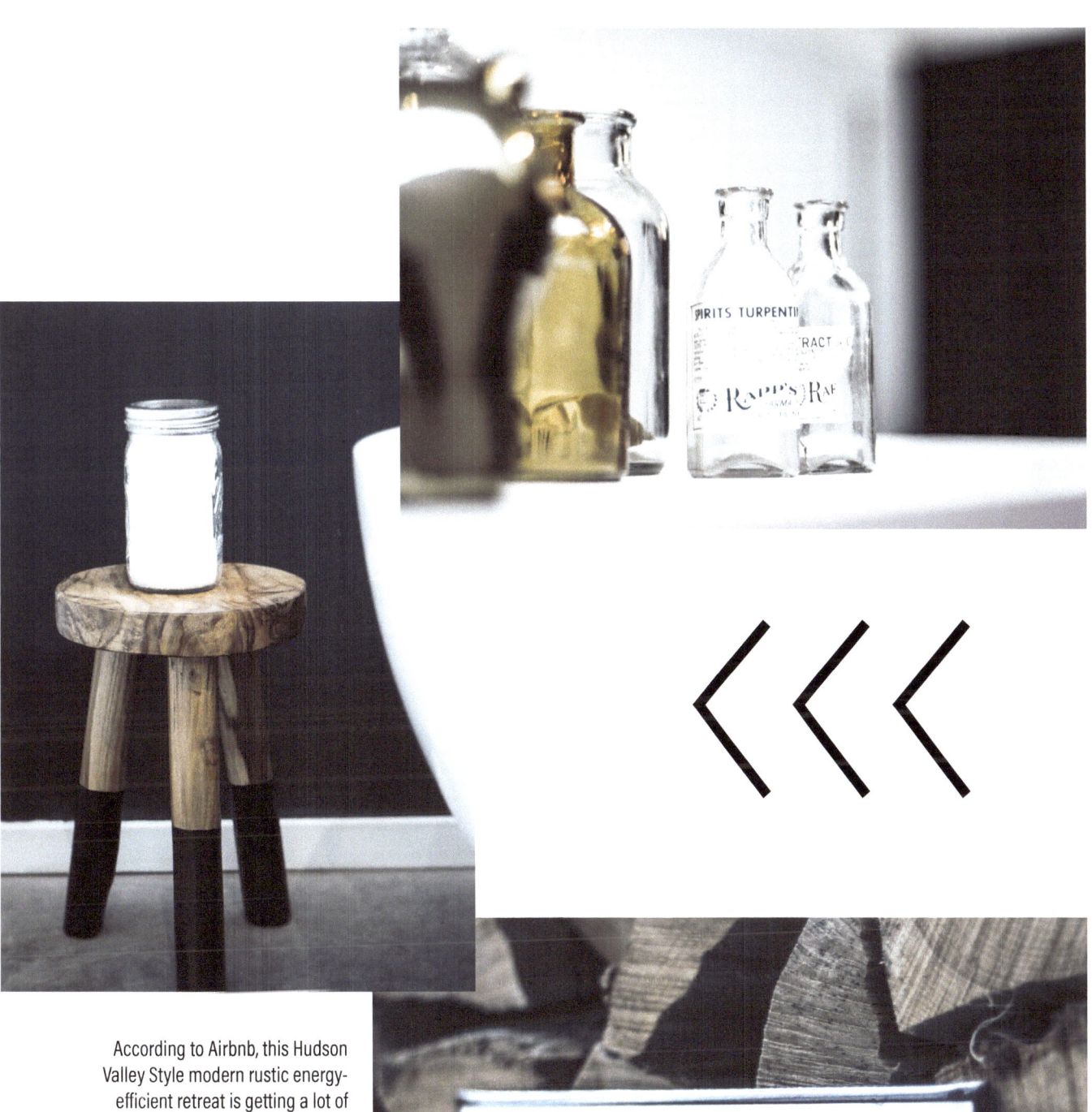

According to Airbnb, this Hudson Valley Style modern rustic energy-efficient retreat is getting a lot of attention recently, so check them on the platform in Rhinebeck, NY!

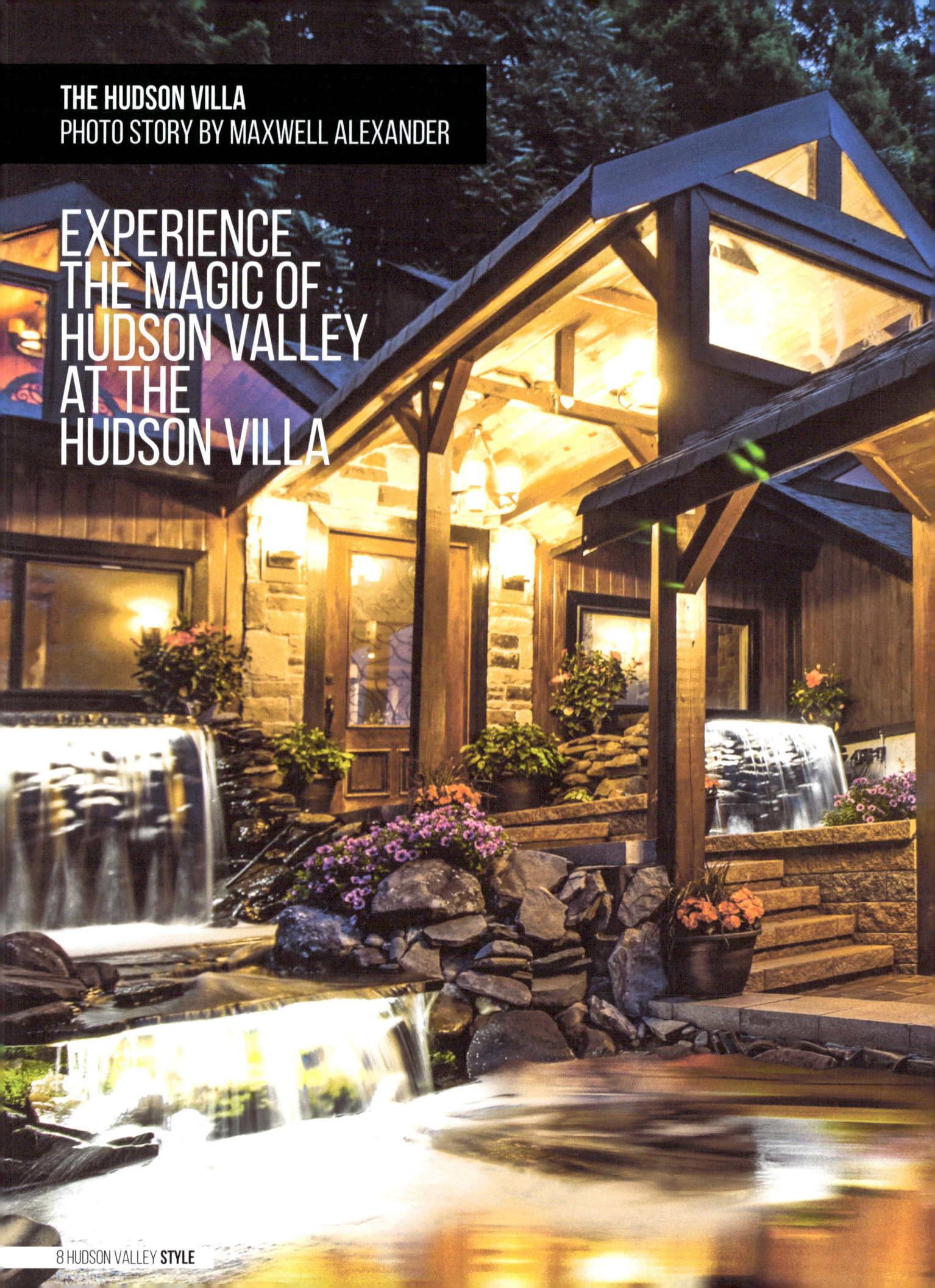

THE HUDSON VILLA
PHOTO STORY BY MAXWELL ALEXANDER

EXPERIENCE THE MAGIC OF HUDSON VALLEY AT THE HUDSON VILLA

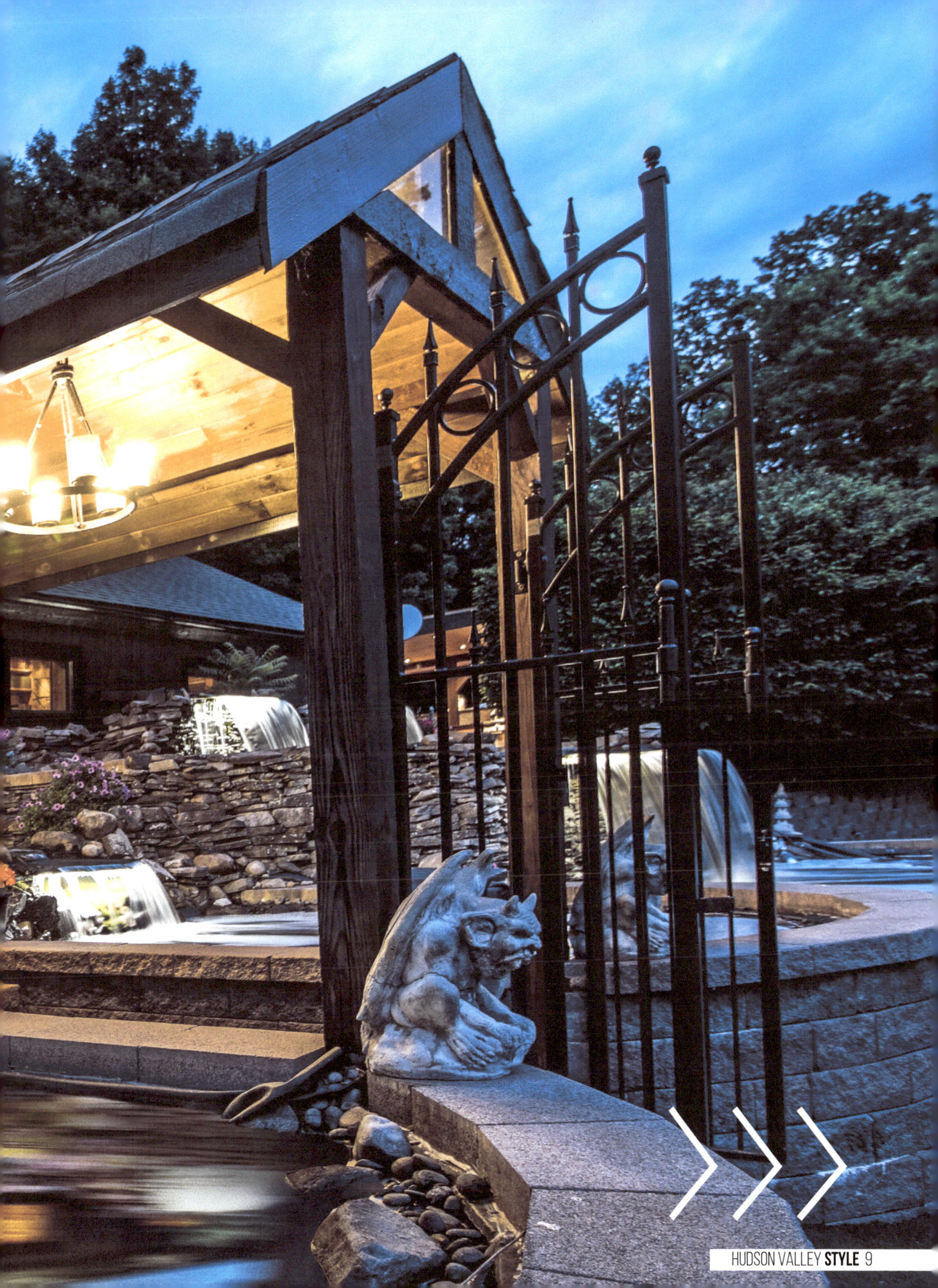

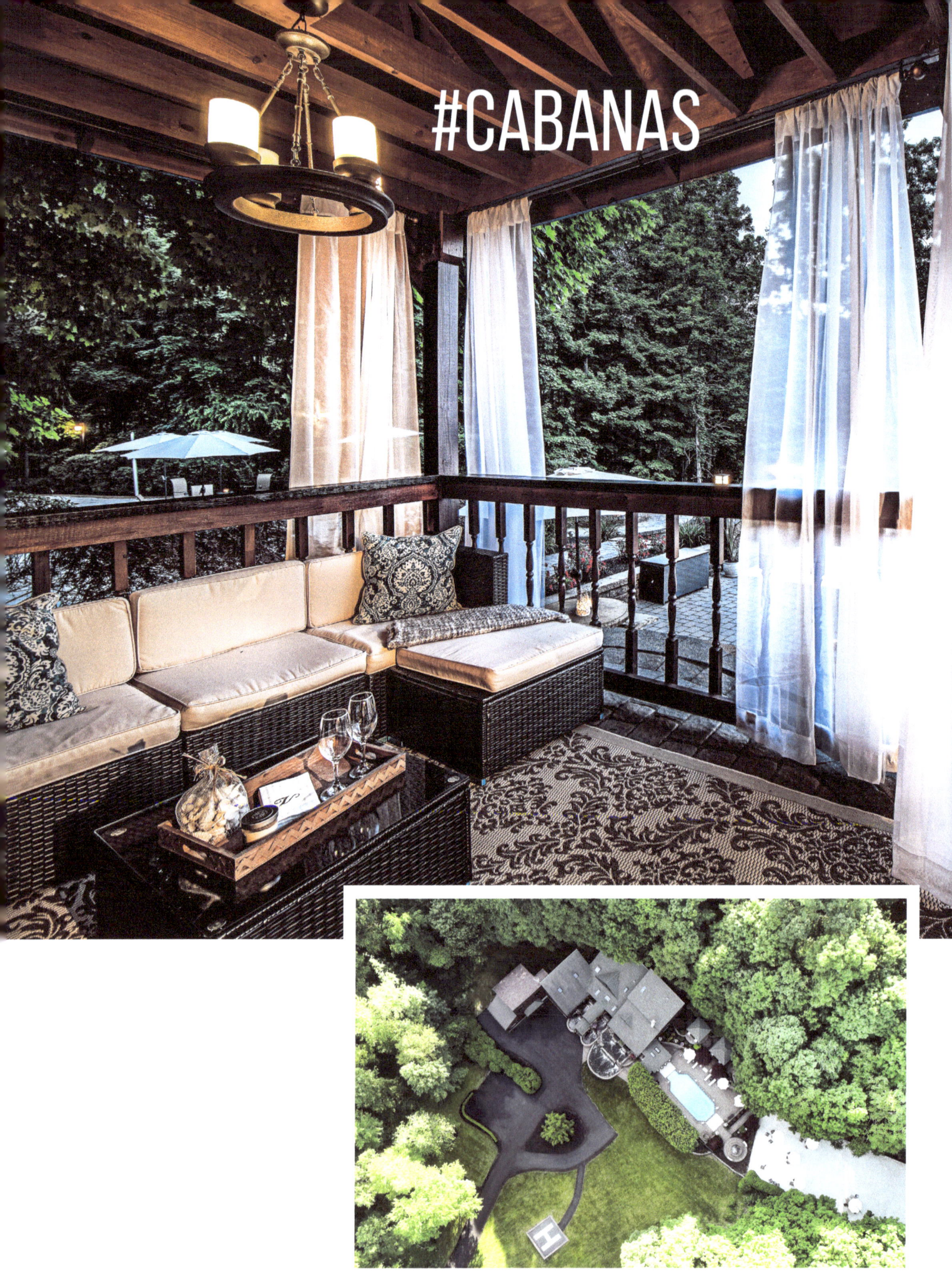

#CABANAS

THE HUDSON VILLA
PHOTO STORY BY MAXWELL ALEXANDER

#BEACH

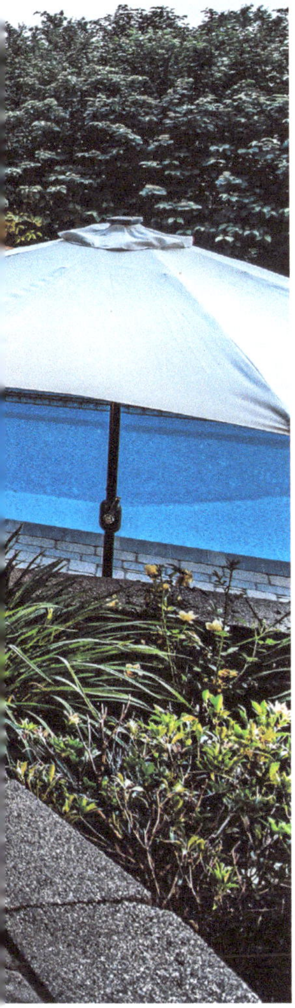

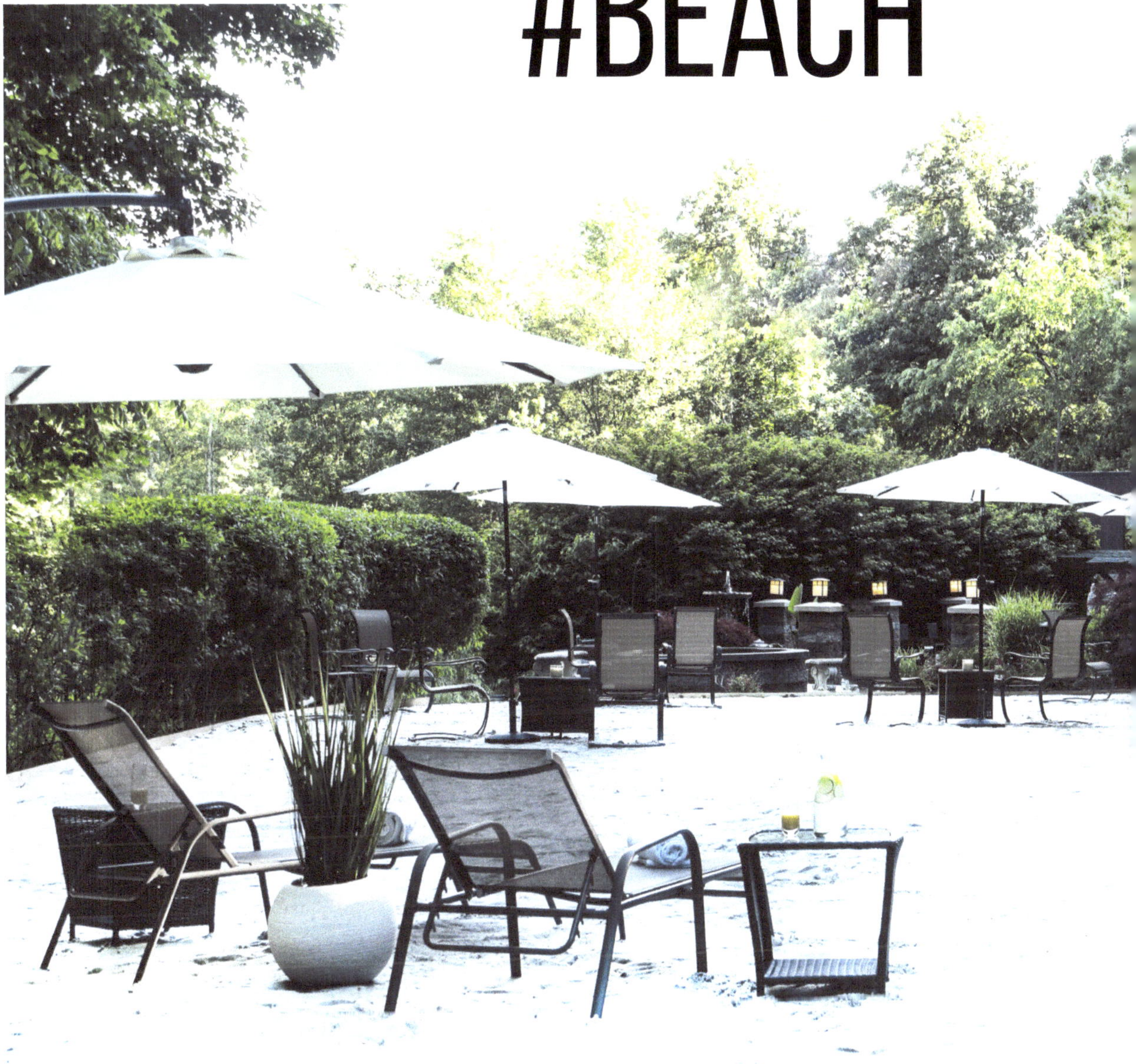

#POOL

>>>

#WATERFALLS

#OUTDOORLIVING

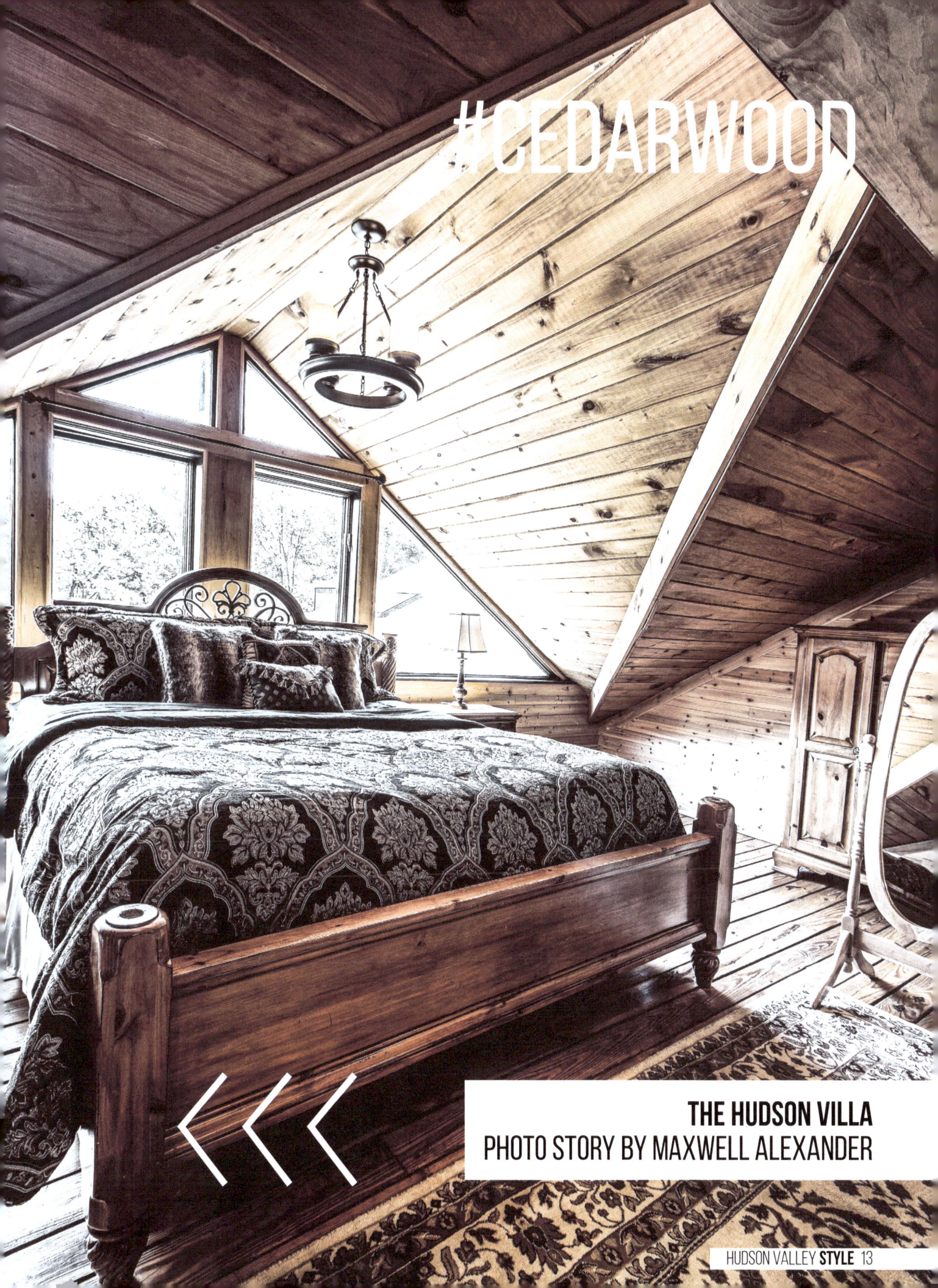

WORKING FROM HOME TIPS
BY KEI KULLBERG

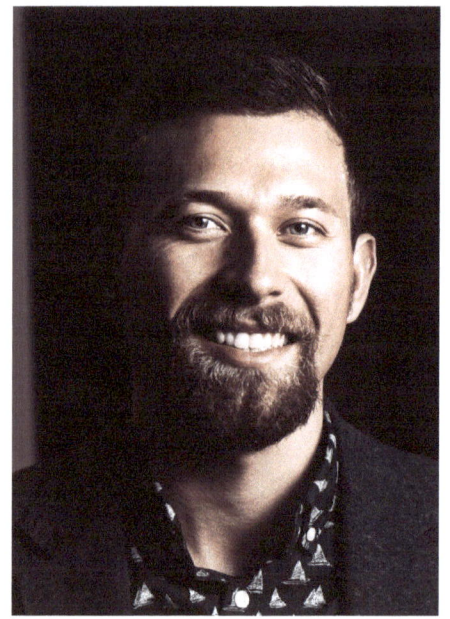

5 AFFORDABLE WAYS TO DRESS UP YOUR HOME OFFICE SPACE

Paid Content by Kei Kullberg, NYS Licensed Mortgage Loan Originator NMLS# 1740248

Spending a lot of time working from home these days? I hear ya! As a mortgage broker here in the Hudson Valley, I see how the area basically turned into a "work-from-home capital" of North-East, just because seems like everyone moved out of New York City...

So the last thing you want is for your home office to look drab. You need a space where you can be excited about starting your workday. Design a home office that will put you in the right headspace for work. You'll want decor that is calming and inviting so that you're eager to begin working every day.

1. A NEW COAT OF PAINT

If you haven't painted in a while, your office walls may look dull and dingy. An easy way to brighten up any room is to give it a new coat of paint. Choose a color that is light and energizing, like a pale yellow or sky blue. You don't want to darken your office as it may lead to you feeling boxed in a small space. Consider adding a fun accent wall to pull the room together. Bold stripes are very popular choices for accent walls; make sure you choose colors that complement each other.

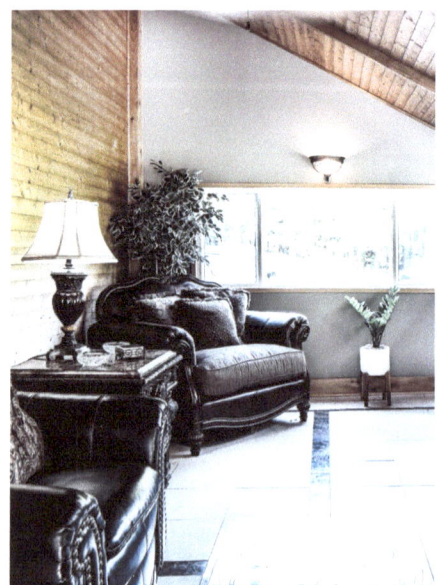

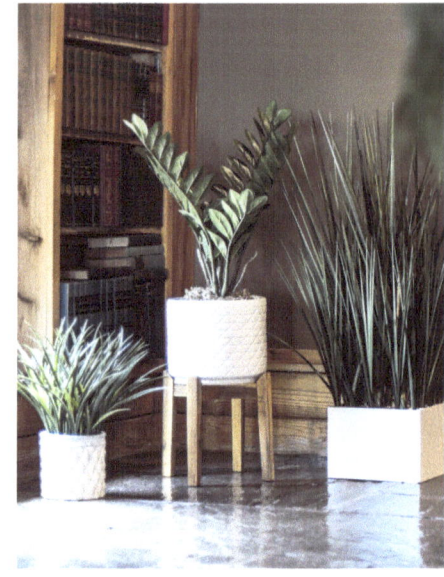

2. HOUSEPLANTS

Liven up your office with a few house plants. House plants are calming and you can water them when your workflow has slowed a bit. You can pick out a wide variety of house plants including ones whose colors complement your office space.

3. INSPIRING WALL ART & MOTIVATIONAL QUOTES

It can be helpful to fill your workspace with inspiring wall art and motivational quotes to keep you going throughout the day. Whether in the form of a poster or a rustic wooden sign, find quotes that inspire you and sprinkle them throughout your office. You can find a lot of motivational decor that suits your interests and decor style online.

4. AN AREA RUG

If you've got a small office, a great way to complete the space is with a large area rug. Not only will a rug pull your room together, but it can add some comfort. Pick a big, fluffy rug to rest your feet on as you get your work done. You may find that making your space cozy will actually help your productivity.

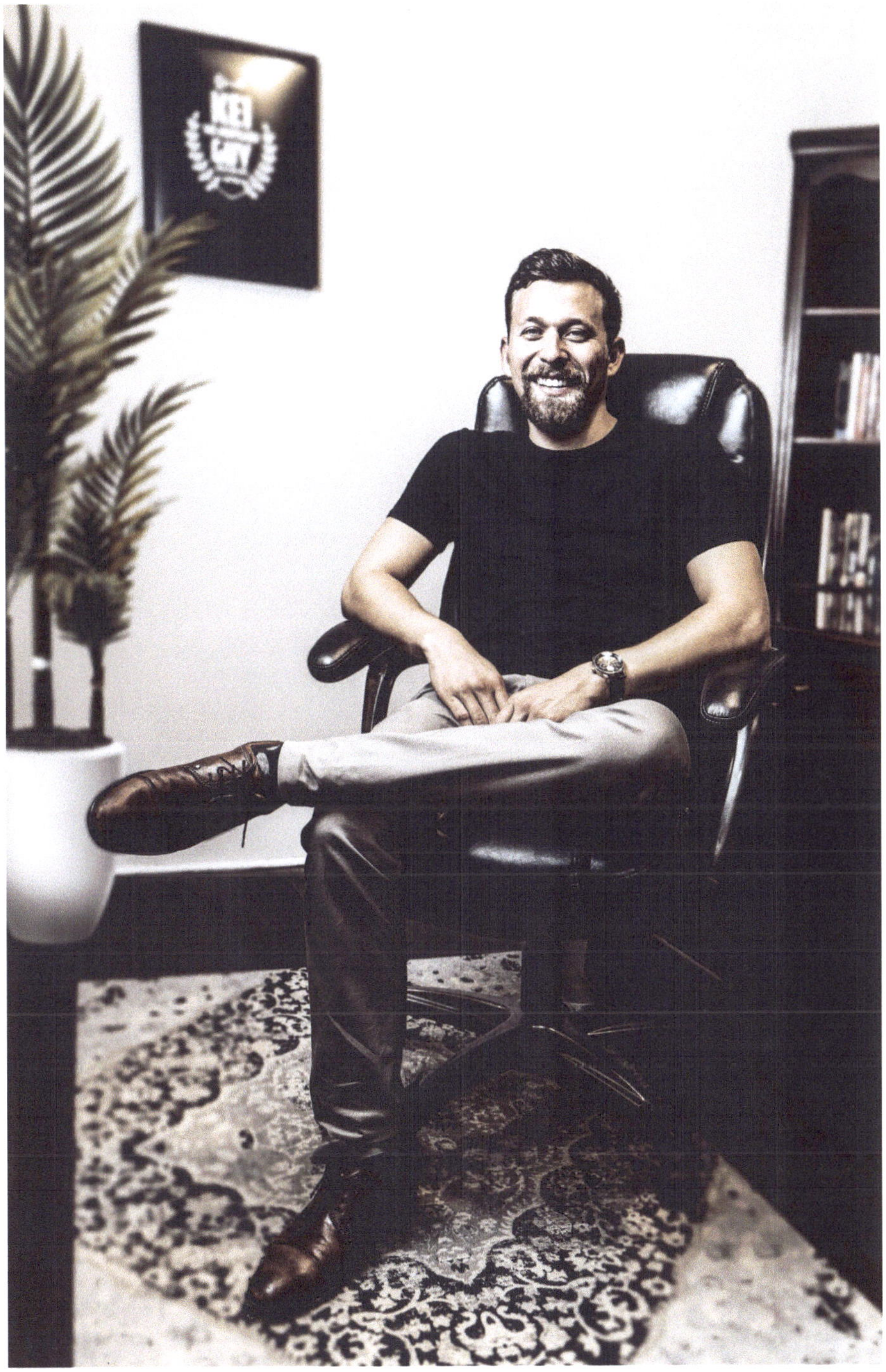

5. PHOTOS OF FRIENDS AND FAMILY

Sometimes when your motivation is running dry, it can be helpful to remember why you are working hard. Perhaps you're working to make your parents proud, to provide a good life for your children, or even just to buy luxury items for your pets. Pick your favorite photos of your loved ones and choose cute frames to keep them on your walls or desk.

Your workspace does not need to drag you down. Create an office you actually enjoy spending your time in by making a few small, affordable changes. Having an office you love will greatly improve your workday.

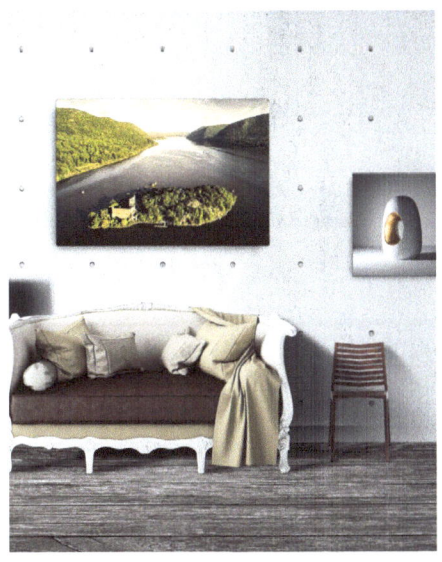

SUMMER PARADISE IN THE HUDSON VALLEY

PHOTO STORY BY MAXWELL ALEXANDER

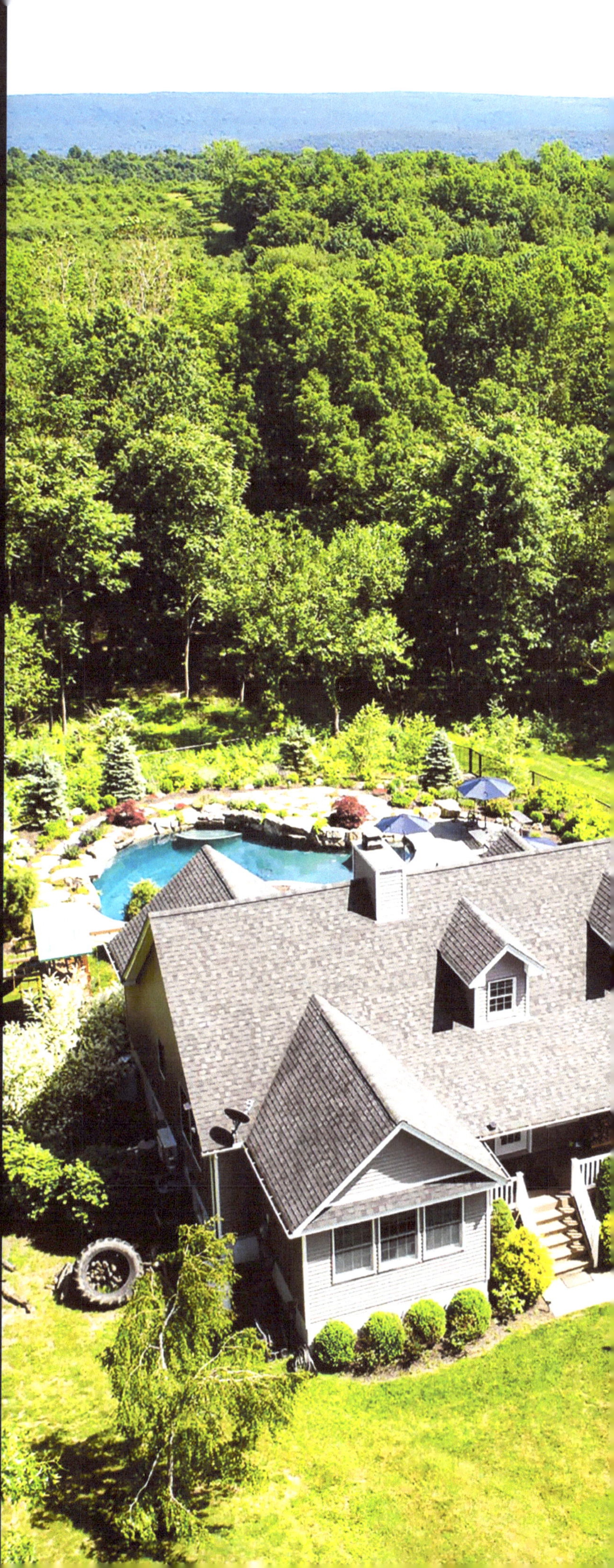

This photoshoot literally took more than 6 months to accomplish, just because summer is not a permanent thing in the Hudson Valley. In fact, I know a lot of people who weather the winter months in warmer climates such as Florida in the US or Caribbean Islands for those who are even luckier.

Well, for those who can still bear the snow and frigid temperatures here in the Modern Rustic Capital of the World, we can only dream of the warmer weather, so please enjoy this warm and fuzzy photo story from Rock Tavern, New York!

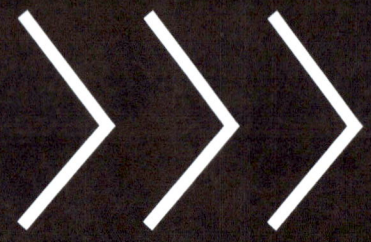

SUMMER PARADISE IN THE HUDSON VALLEY
PHOTO STORY BY MAXWELL ALEXANDER

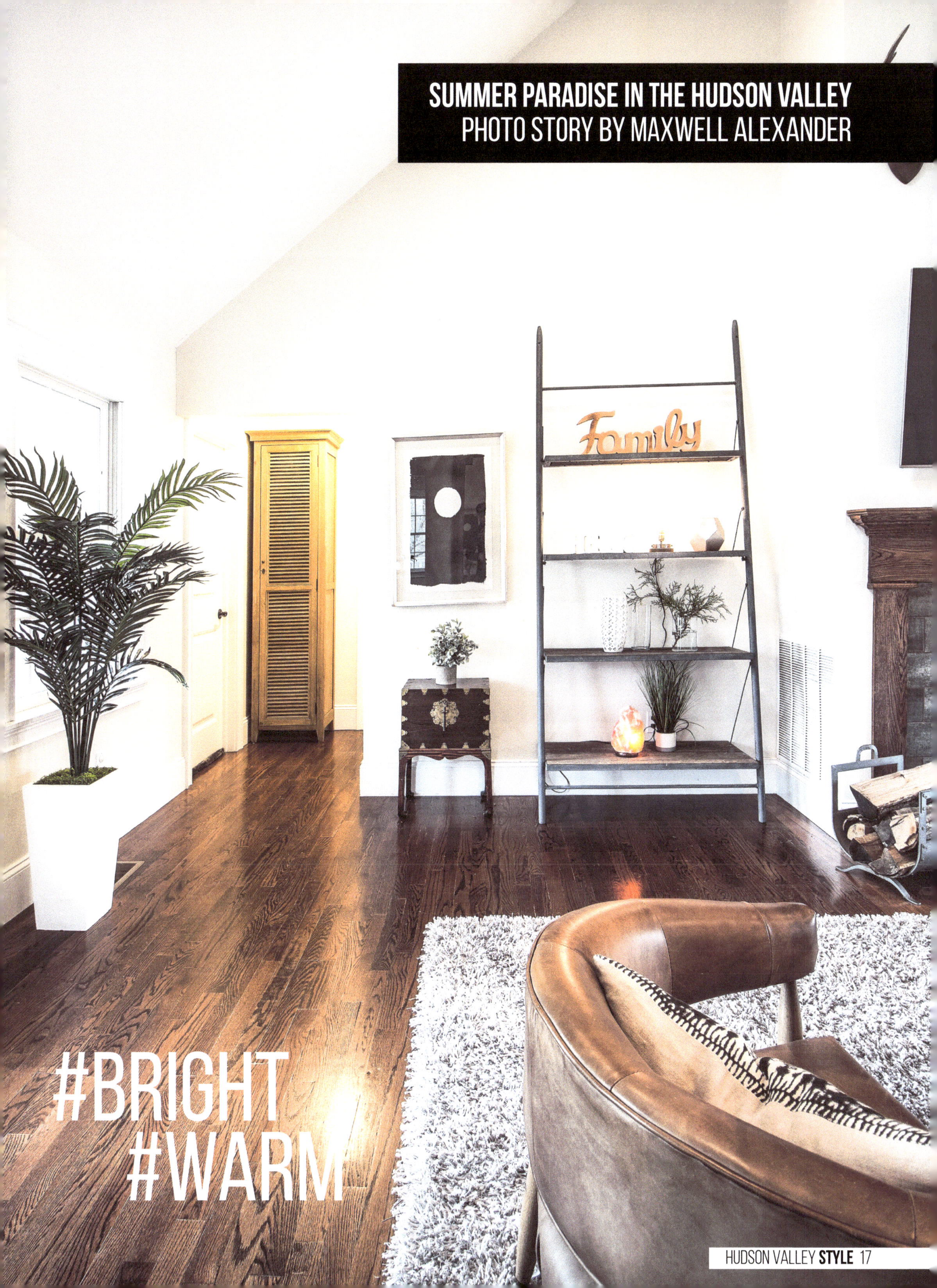

#BRIGHT
#WARM

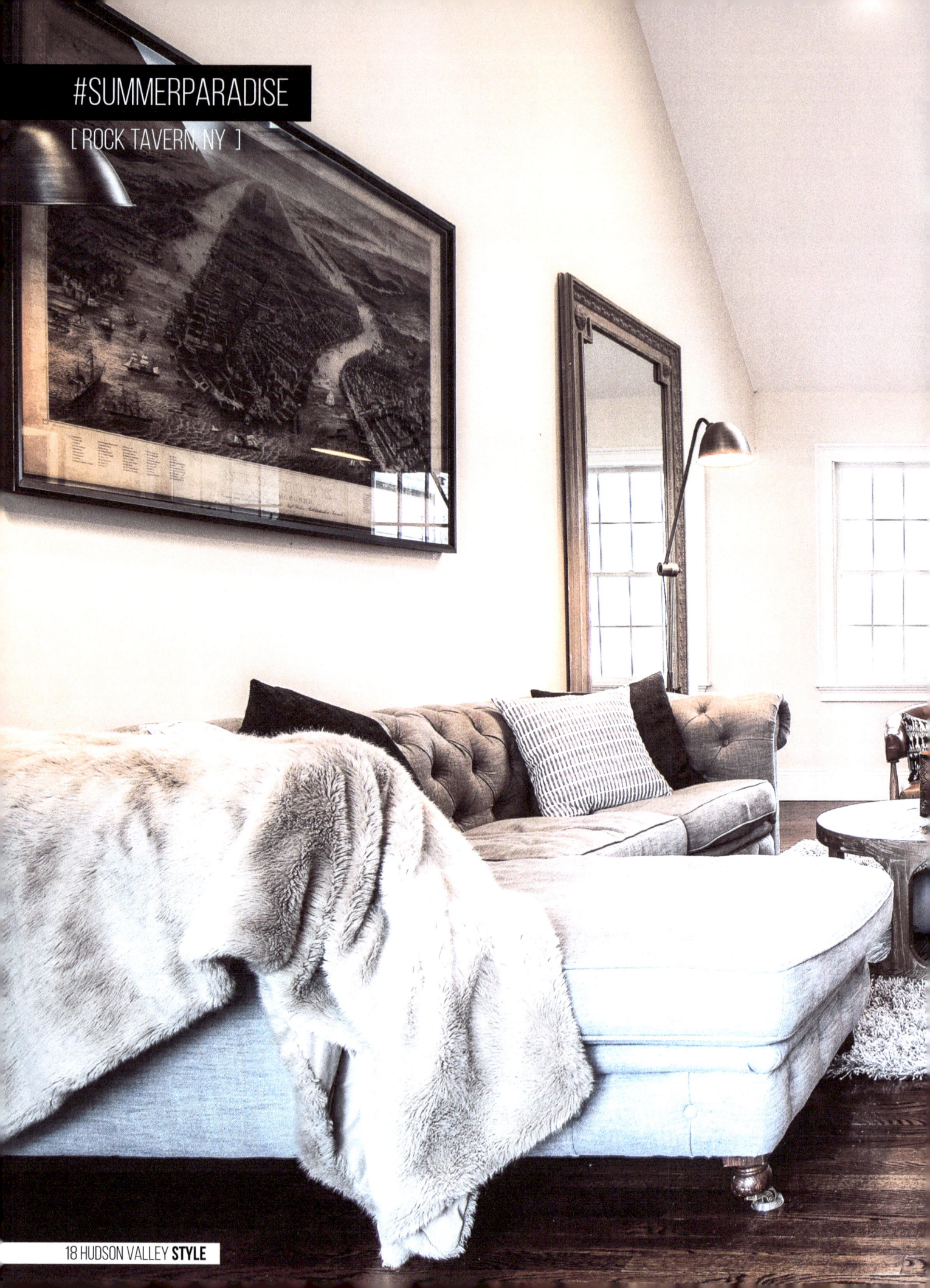

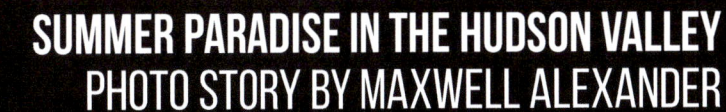

SUMMER PARADISE IN THE HUDSON VALLEY
PHOTO STORY BY MAXWELL ALEXANDER

#MODERN
#AUTHENTIC
#RUSTIC

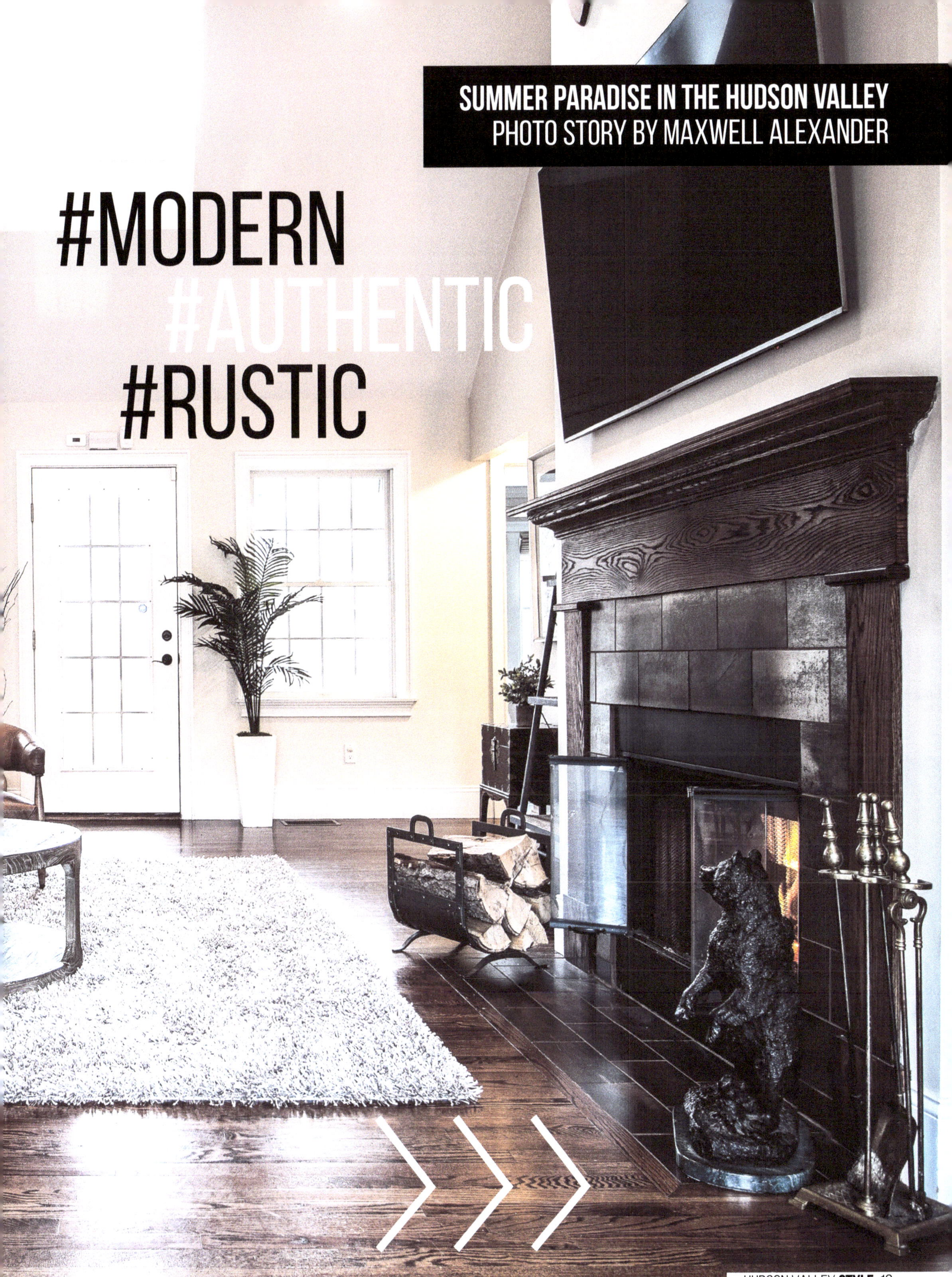

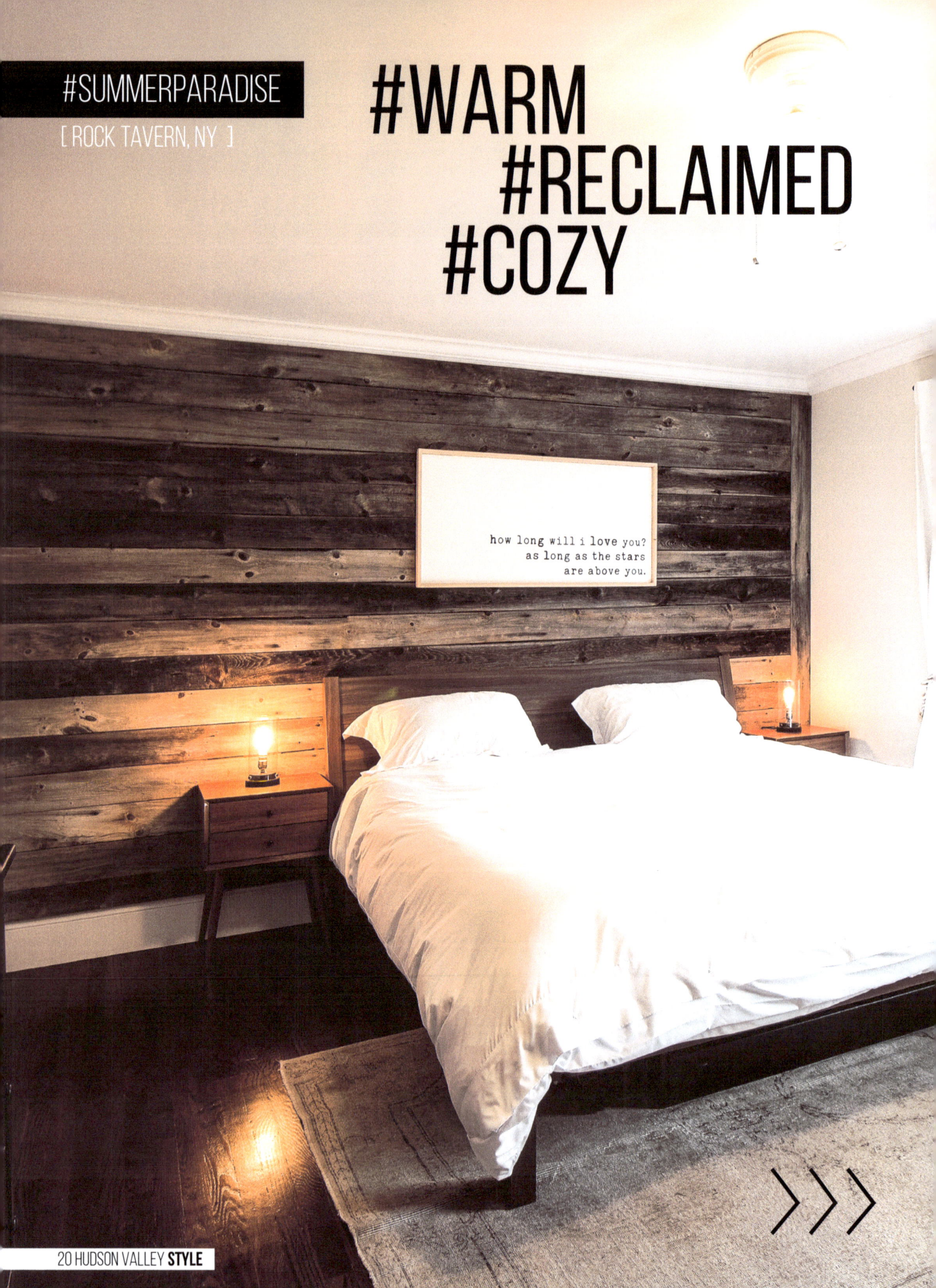

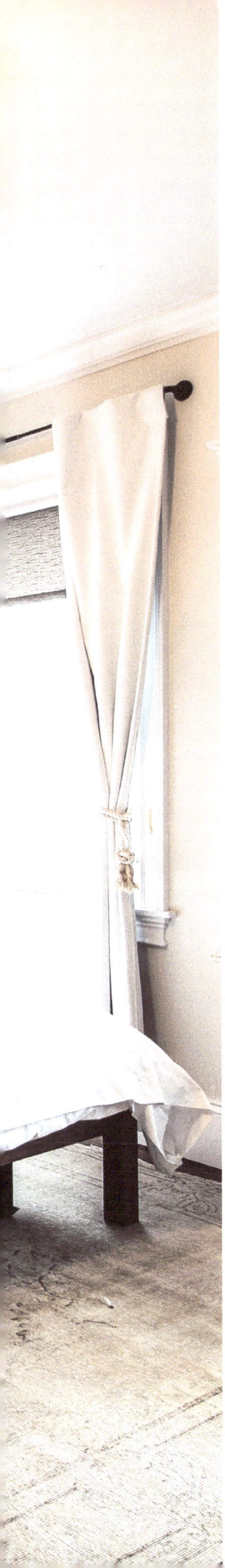

SUMMER PARADISE IN THE HUDSON VALLEY
PHOTO STORY BY MAXWELL ALEXANDER

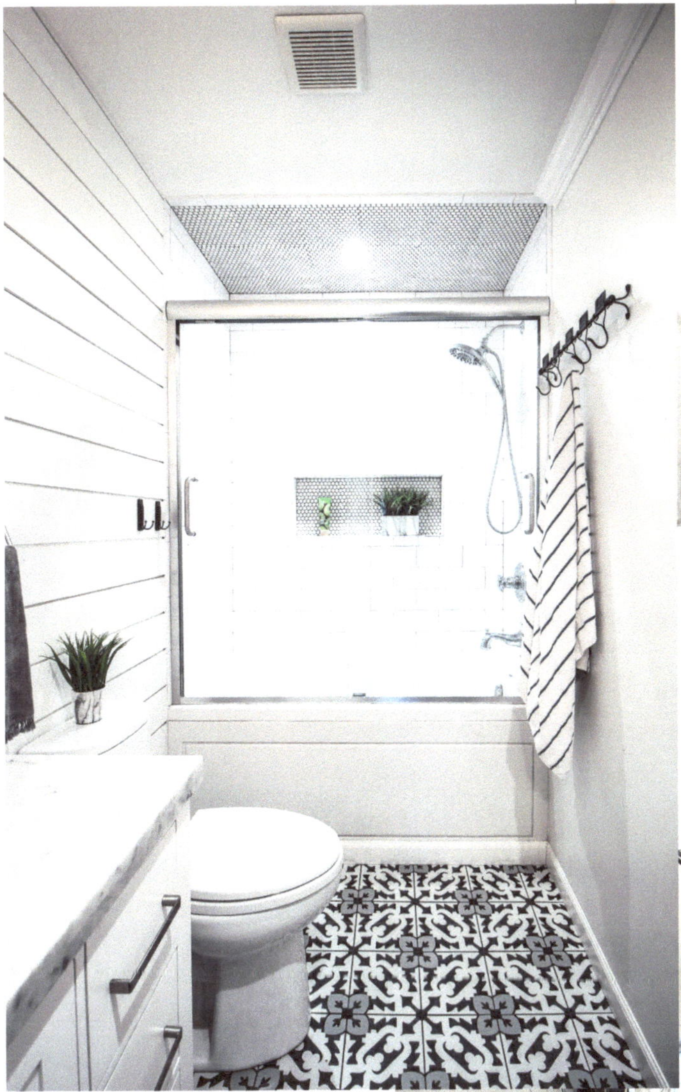

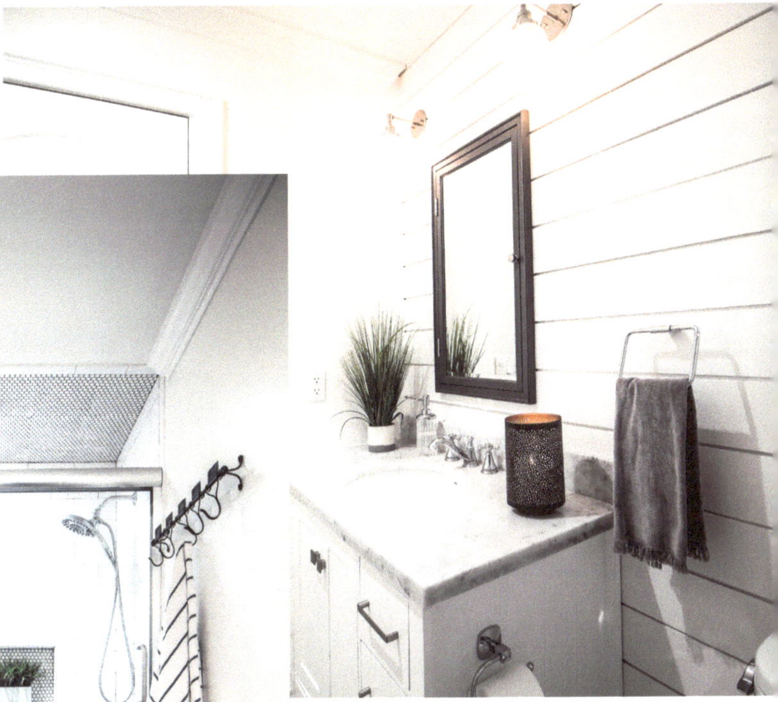

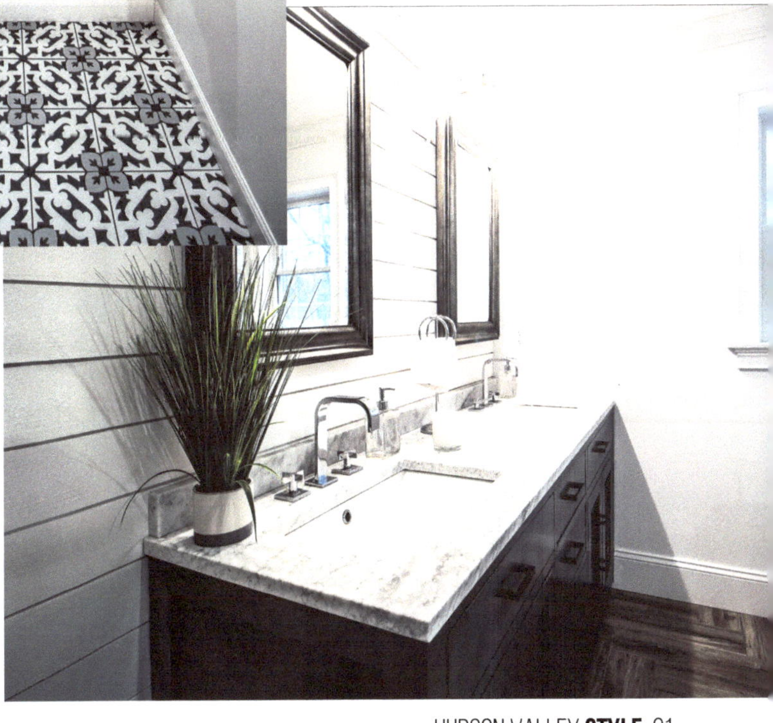

#WHITE #CLEAN #SHIPLAP

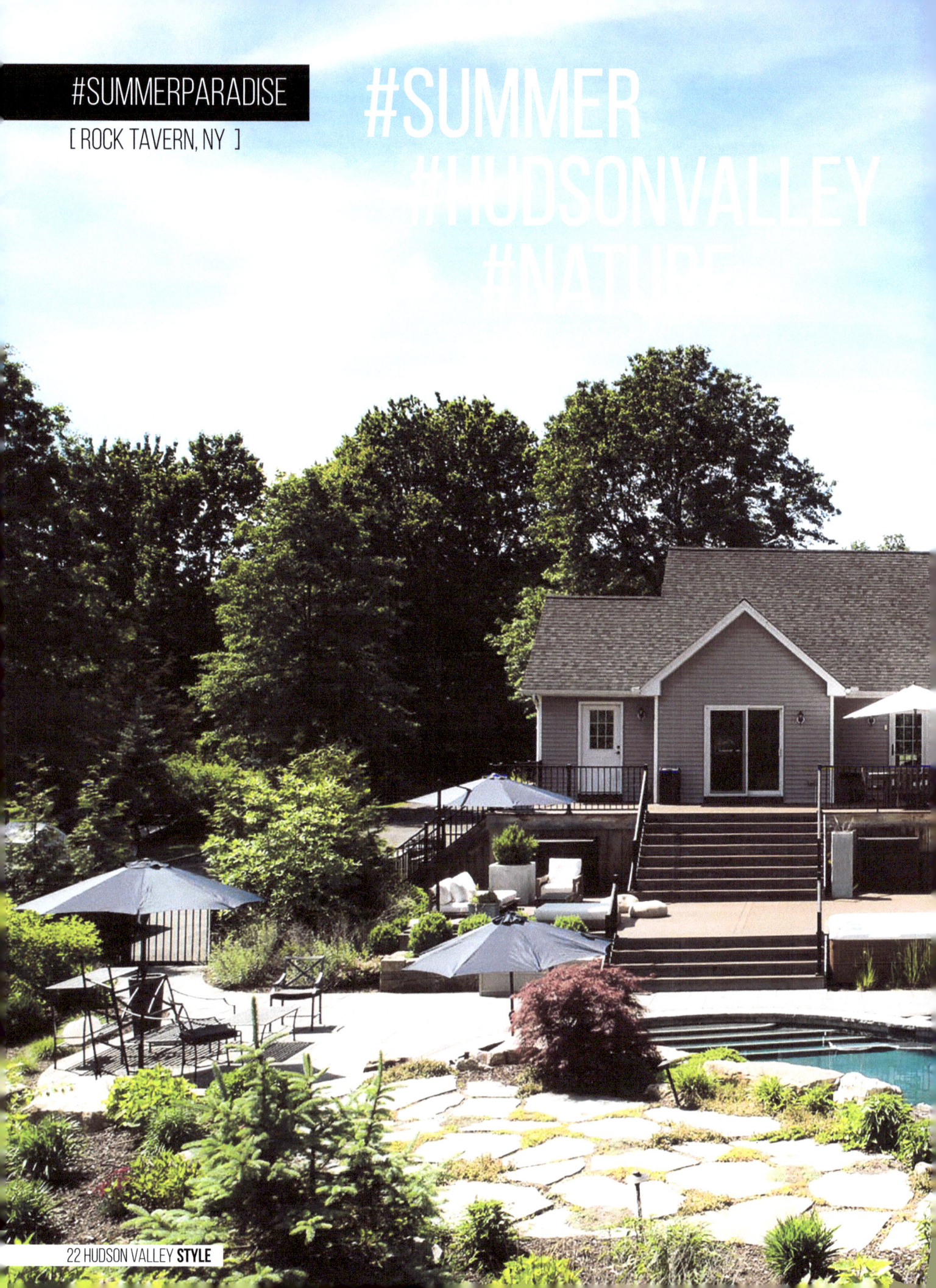

#SUMMERPARADISE
[ROCK TAVERN, NY]

#SUMMER
#HUDSONVALLEY
#NATURE

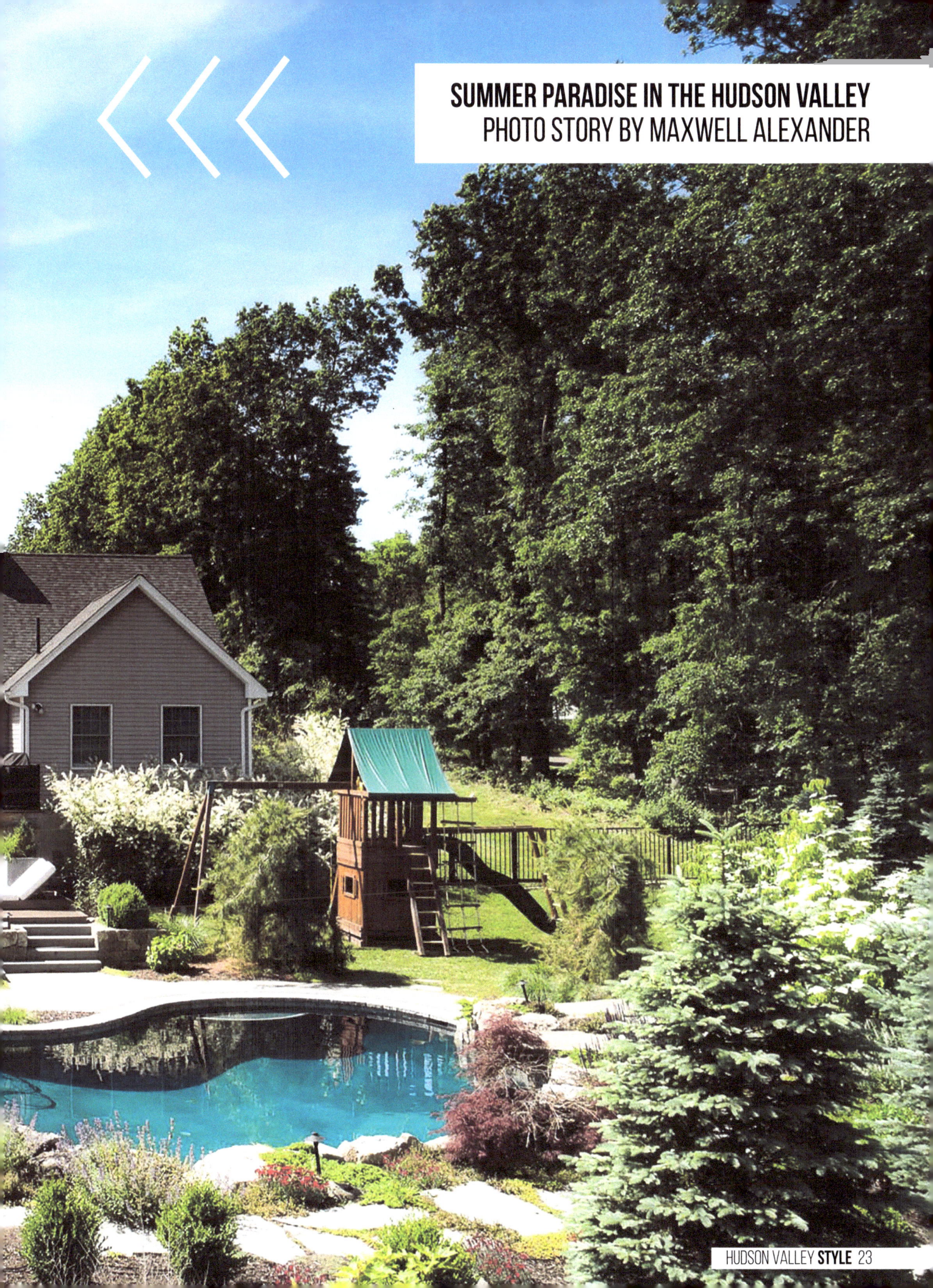

SUMMER PARADISE IN THE HUDSON VALLEY
PHOTO STORY BY MAXWELL ALEXANDER

simplida™

[world's finest wall art]

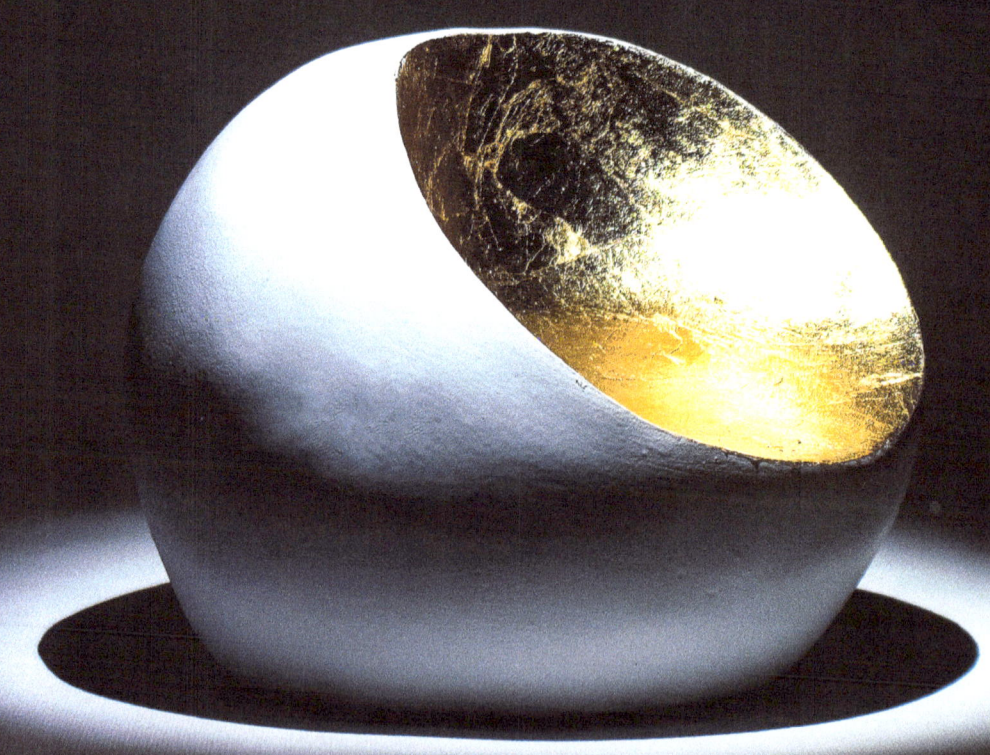

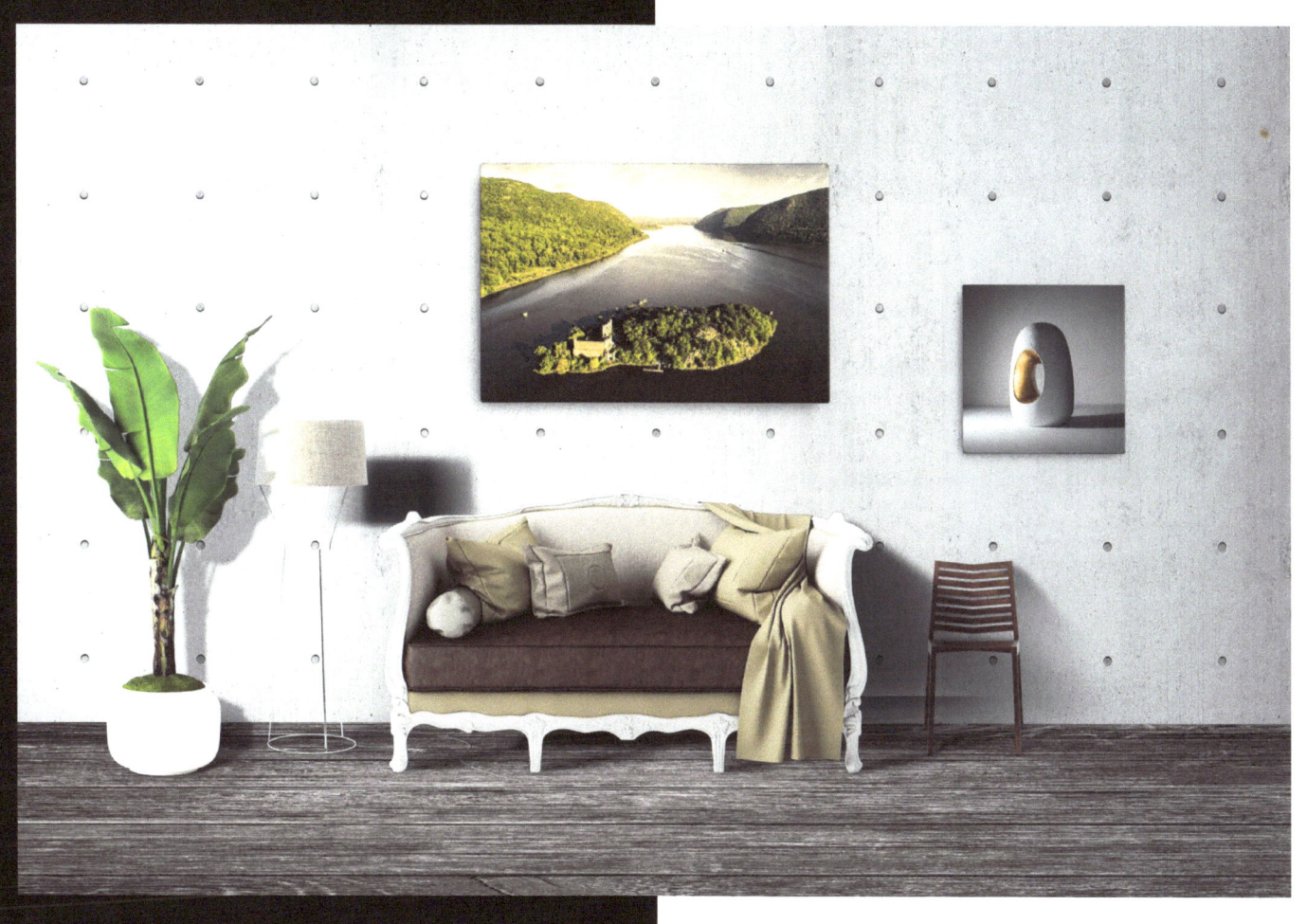

USE
PROMO CODE:
HVSTYLE30
FOR 30% OFF
ALL CANVAS PRINTS
AT SIMPLIDA.COM

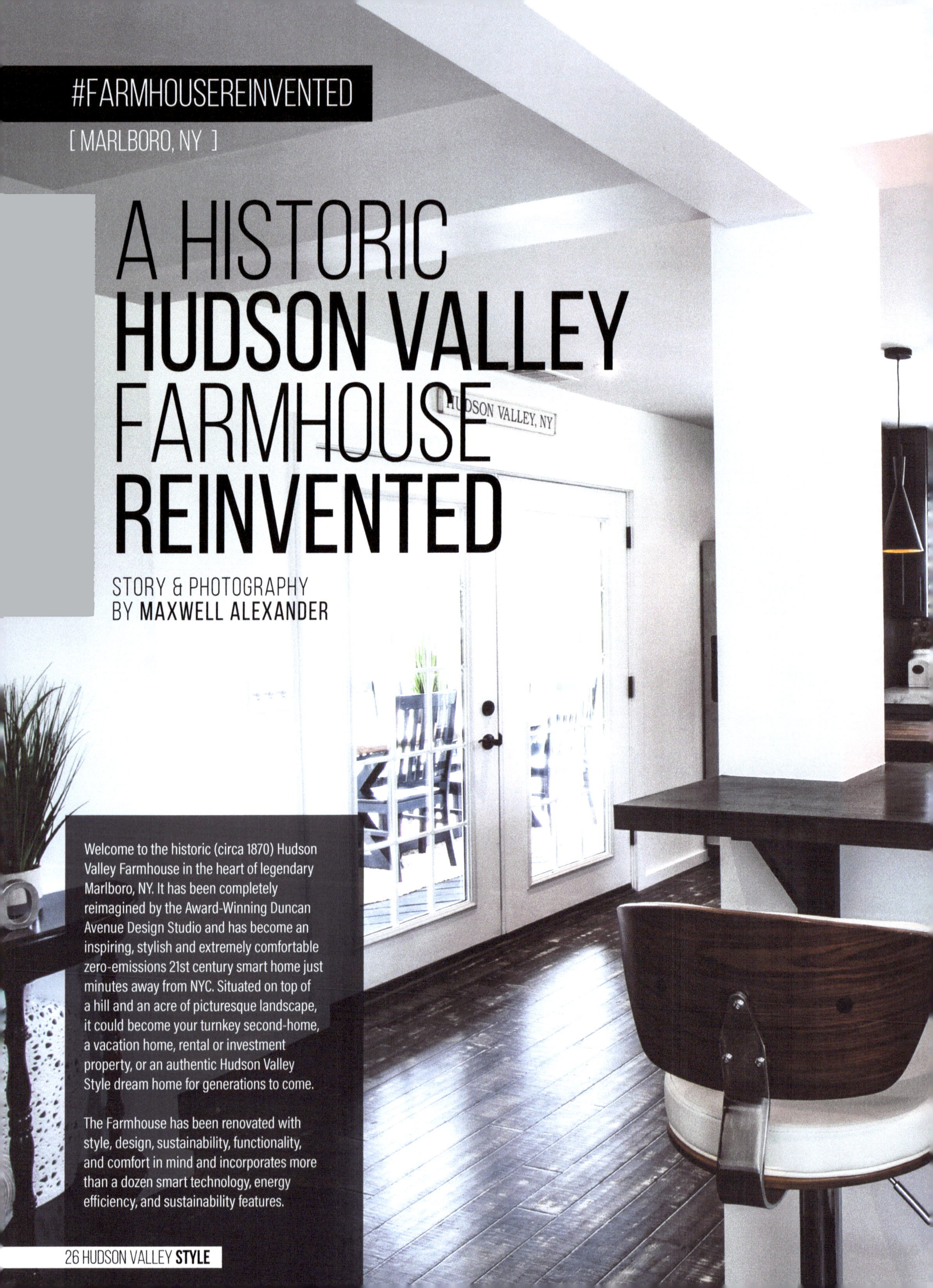

#FARMHOUSEREINVENTED
[MARLBORO, NY]

A HISTORIC HUDSON VALLEY FARMHOUSE REINVENTED

STORY & PHOTOGRAPHY BY **MAXWELL ALEXANDER**

Welcome to the historic (circa 1870) Hudson Valley Farmhouse in the heart of legendary Marlboro, NY. It has been completely reimagined by the Award-Winning Duncan Avenue Design Studio and has become an inspiring, stylish and extremely comfortable zero-emissions 21st century smart home just minutes away from NYC. Situated on top of a hill and an acre of picturesque landscape, it could become your turnkey second-home, a vacation home, rental or investment property, or an authentic Hudson Valley Style dream home for generations to come.

The Farmhouse has been renovated with style, design, sustainability, functionality, and comfort in mind and incorporates more than a dozen smart technology, energy efficiency, and sustainability features.

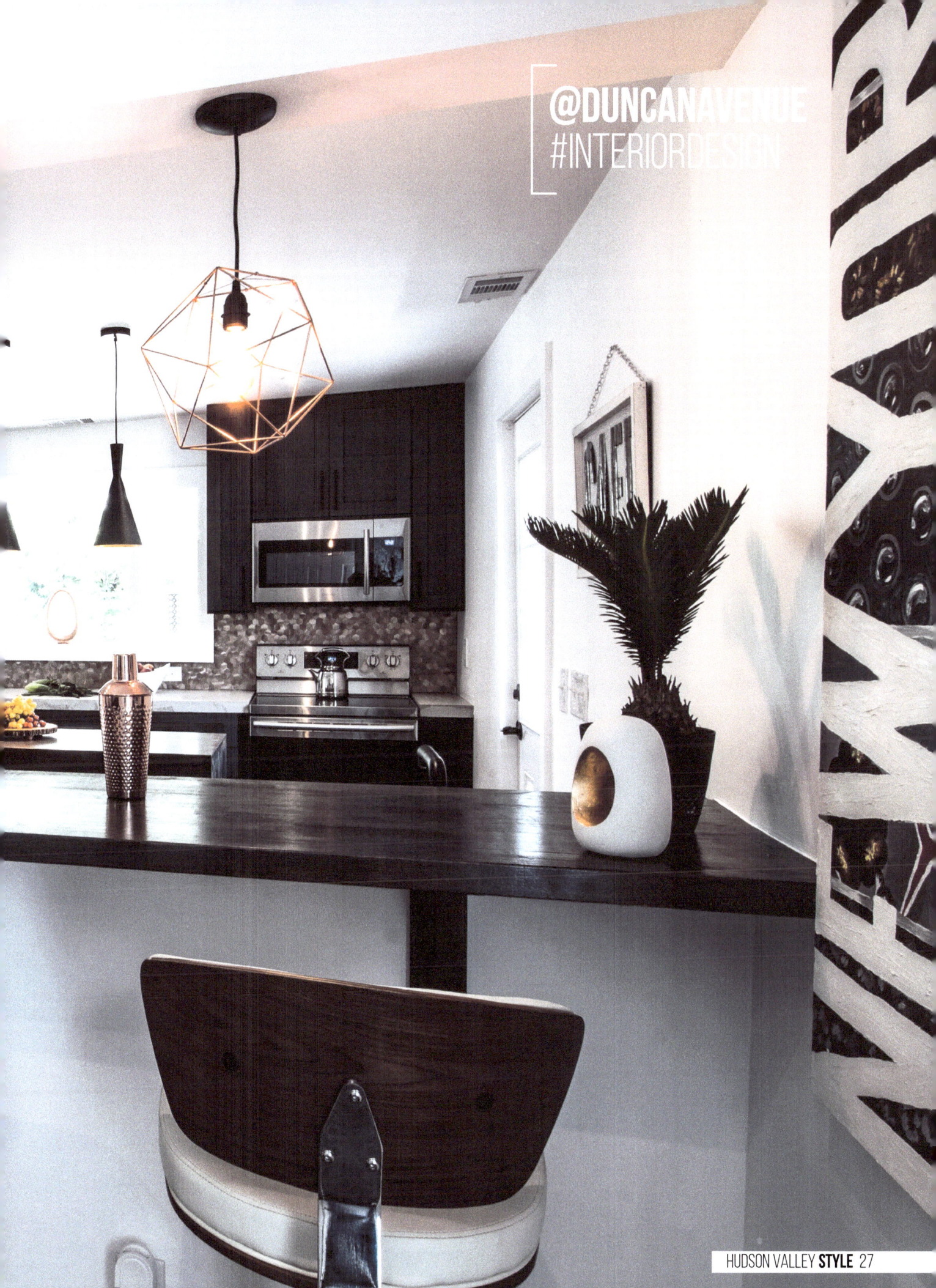

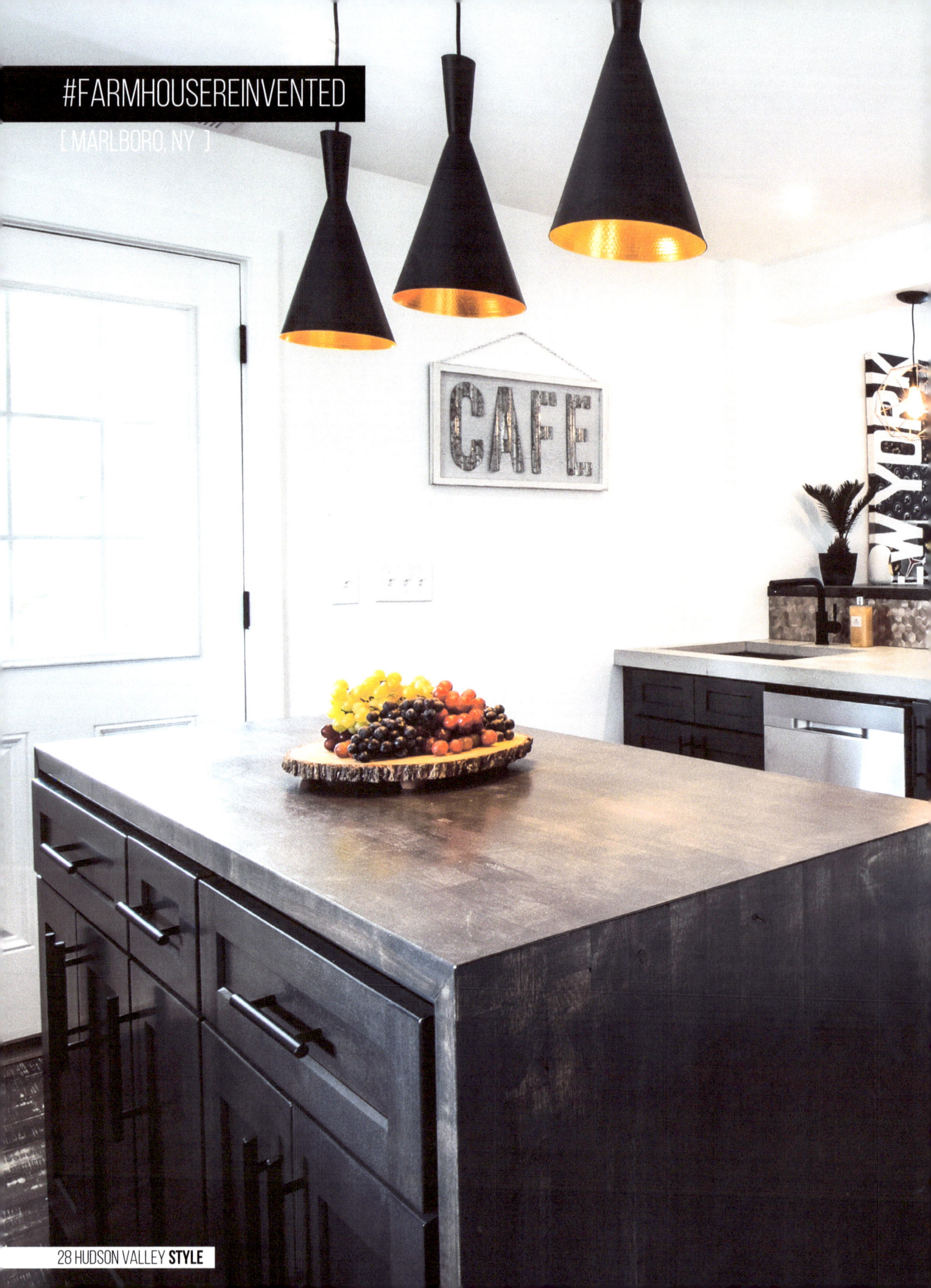

CONTEMPORARY SMART FLOOR PLAN

Contemporary open concept floorplan, glass french doors and 210° wraparound porch with 3-season outdoor dining space blur the line between indoor and outdoor living and allow residents and guests to enjoy a true connection with surrounding nature.

Wake up to the sunrise shining through double glass doors on the east side of the house and watch the warm sunset rays shining through plenty of energy-efficient windows and french doors on the west. High-end finishes such as sustainable bamboo hardwood floors, sustainable concrete countertops, solid wood kitchen cabinets with soft closing drawers, energy star stainless steel appliances, and designer light fixtures are only a few of the updates along with a brand-new central HVAC heat pump system controlled by smart Nest thermostat with two-zone sensors.

Brand new roof, utilities, and all LED lighting bring additional value and comfort for many years to come. The property features a beautiful designer pergola on the edge of the hill with an opportunity for the in-ground infinity pool. Property's sun number is 91 and is all set for installation of your own solar farm that will take the property go 100% off-grid.

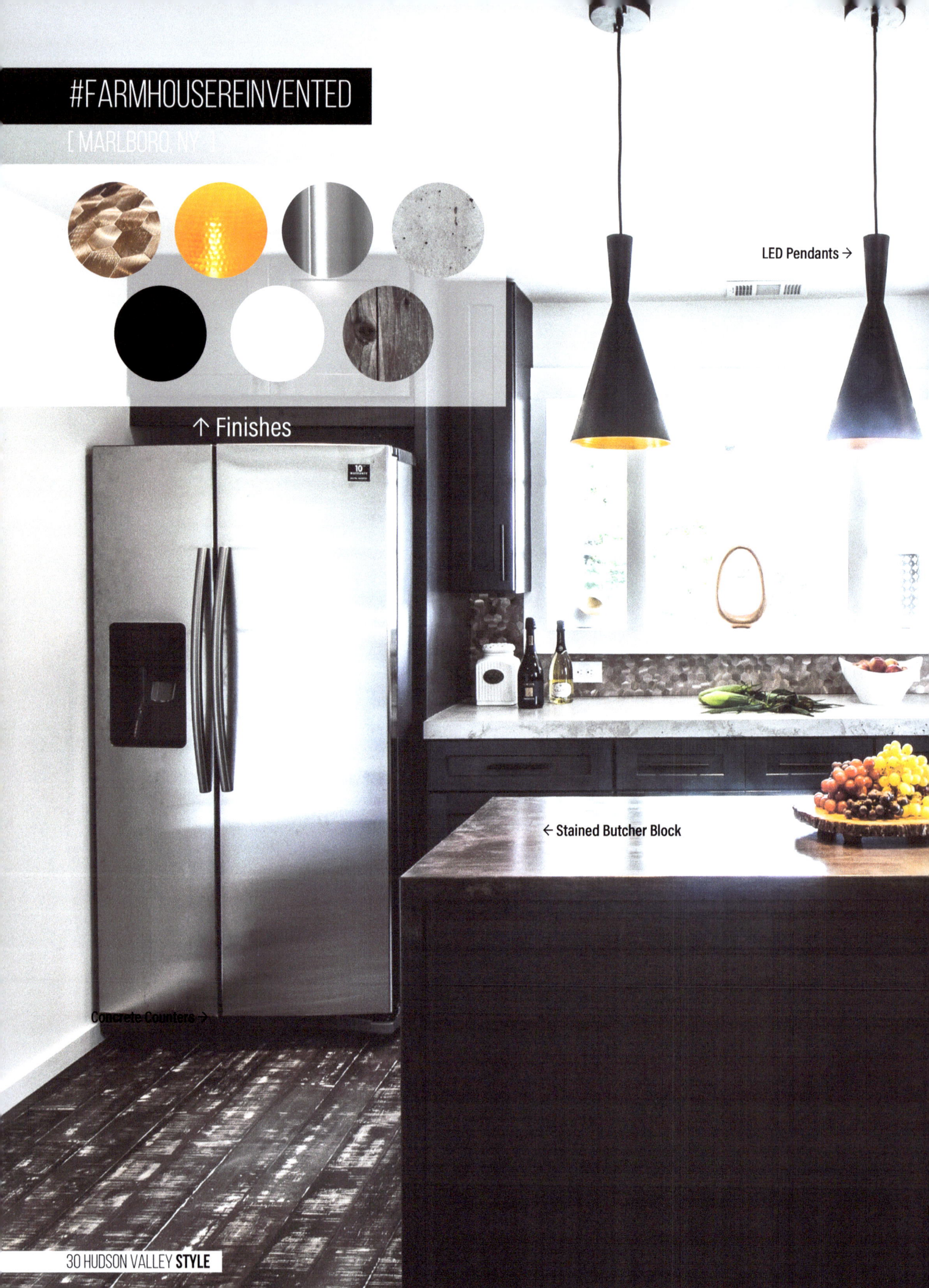

#FARMHOUSEREINVENTED
[MARLBORO, NY]

↑ Finishes

LED Pendants →

← Stained Butcher Block

Concrete Counters →

30 HUDSON VALLEY **STYLE**

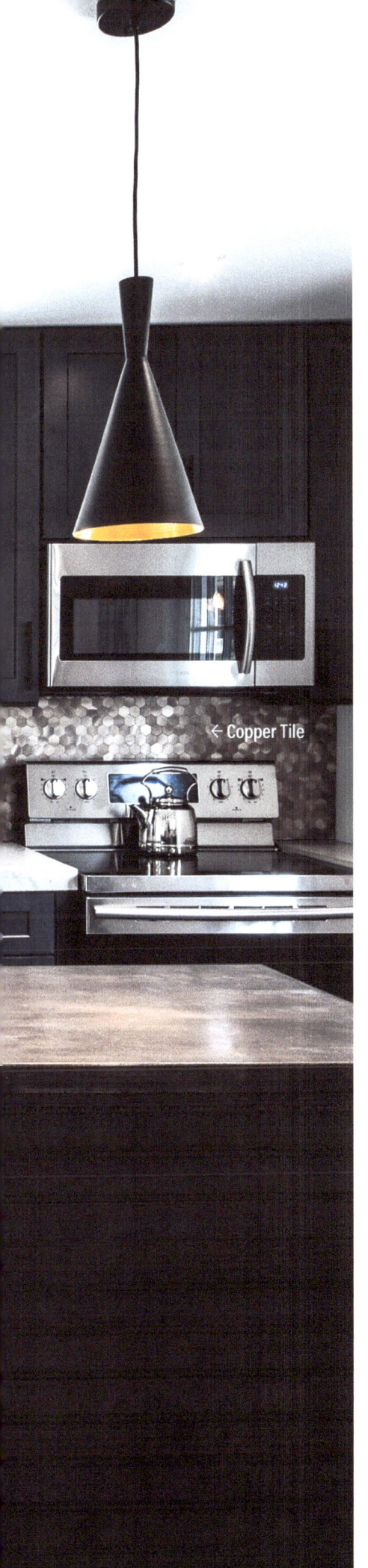

← Copper Tile

SUSTAINABLE CONCRETE & WOOD COUNTERTOPS

This kitchen has a lot of character thanks to the sophisticated/industrial look of concrete countertops. They are not just trendy, but also environmentally-friendly. One of the unique characteristics of concrete is that this material will evolve and adopt character over time, so the appearance of your counters will improve with age. Concrete counters are durable and heat-resistant for all of you avid bakers out there. The material is non-toxic, does not emit VOCs unlike plastics/polymers and is a sustainable material, unlike granite or marble. Concrete is a friend of the environment in all stages of its life span, from raw material production to demolition, making it a natural choice for sustainable home construction.

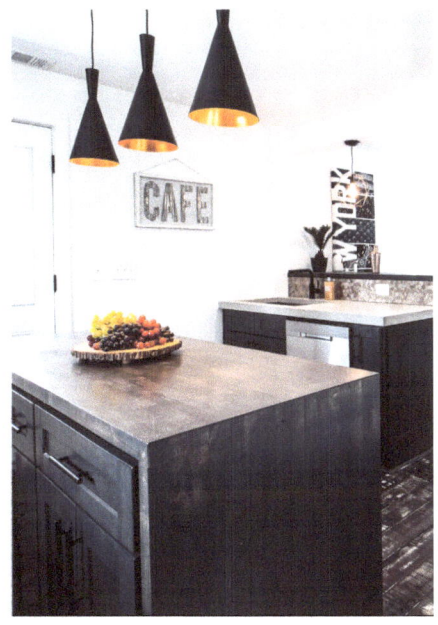

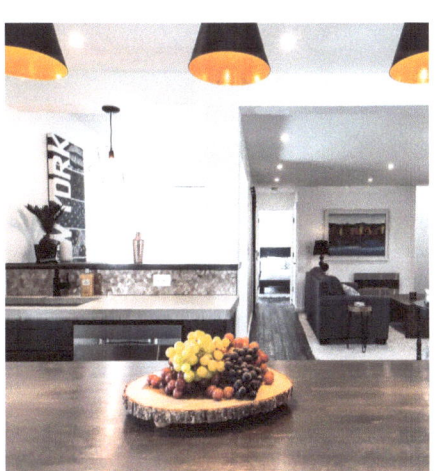

STAINLESS STEEL ENERGY STAR APPLIANCES

Stainless Steel Energy Star Appliances are an important accord in an overall symphony of this amazing and functional kitchen. They are positioned in the most efficient way to ensure an easy cooking process. The kitchen features range hood vented outside of the house and stylish yet environmentally-friendly electric range. Hudson Valley region energy providers offer an option to switch to 100% renewable electricity from wind and solar, so the electric range makes a lot of sense.

#FARMHOUSEREINVENTED
[MARLBORO, NY]

NATURAL PATTERNS CERAMIC TILE MATTE BLACK ACCENTS

Natural look and natural materials. This time we went with darker accents colors, but overall both bathrooms in this house are bright and airy.

FLOATING VANITIES & BARN DOORS, CERAMIC TILE, DESIGNER LED LIGHT FIXTURES, AN ABUNDANCE OF LIGHT & SPACE CREATE AN INSPIRING SPA-LIKE EXPERIENCE

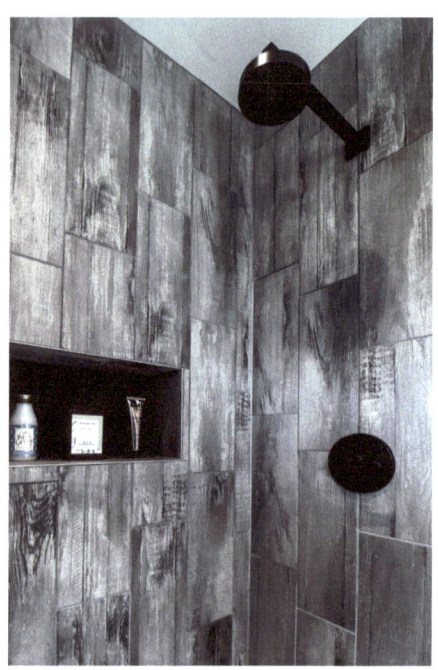

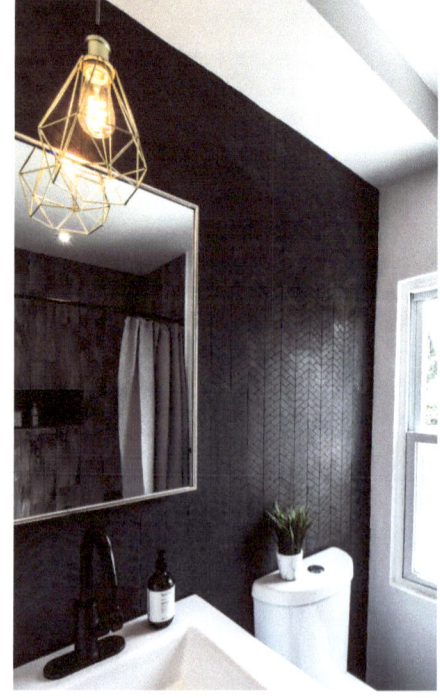

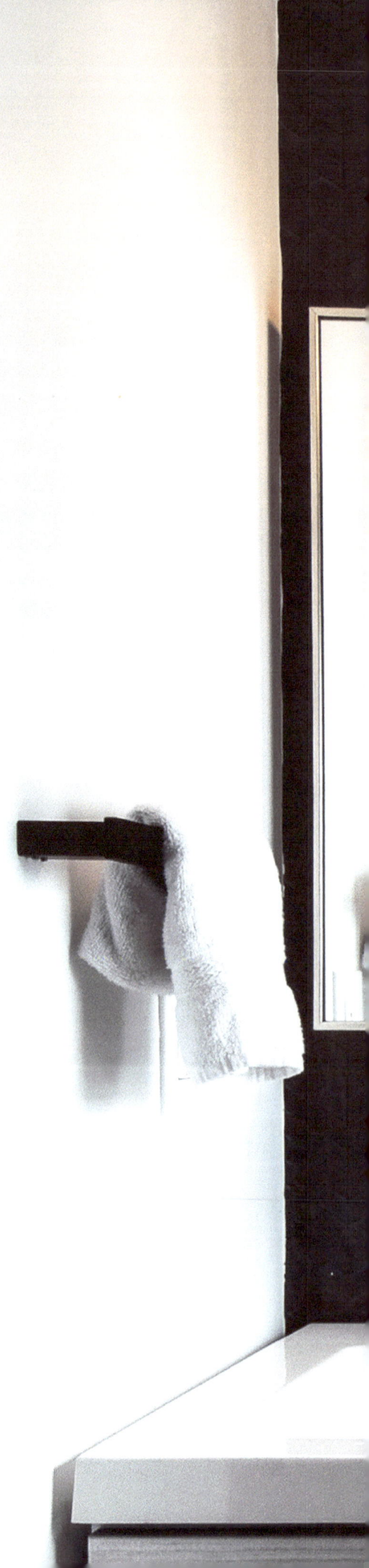

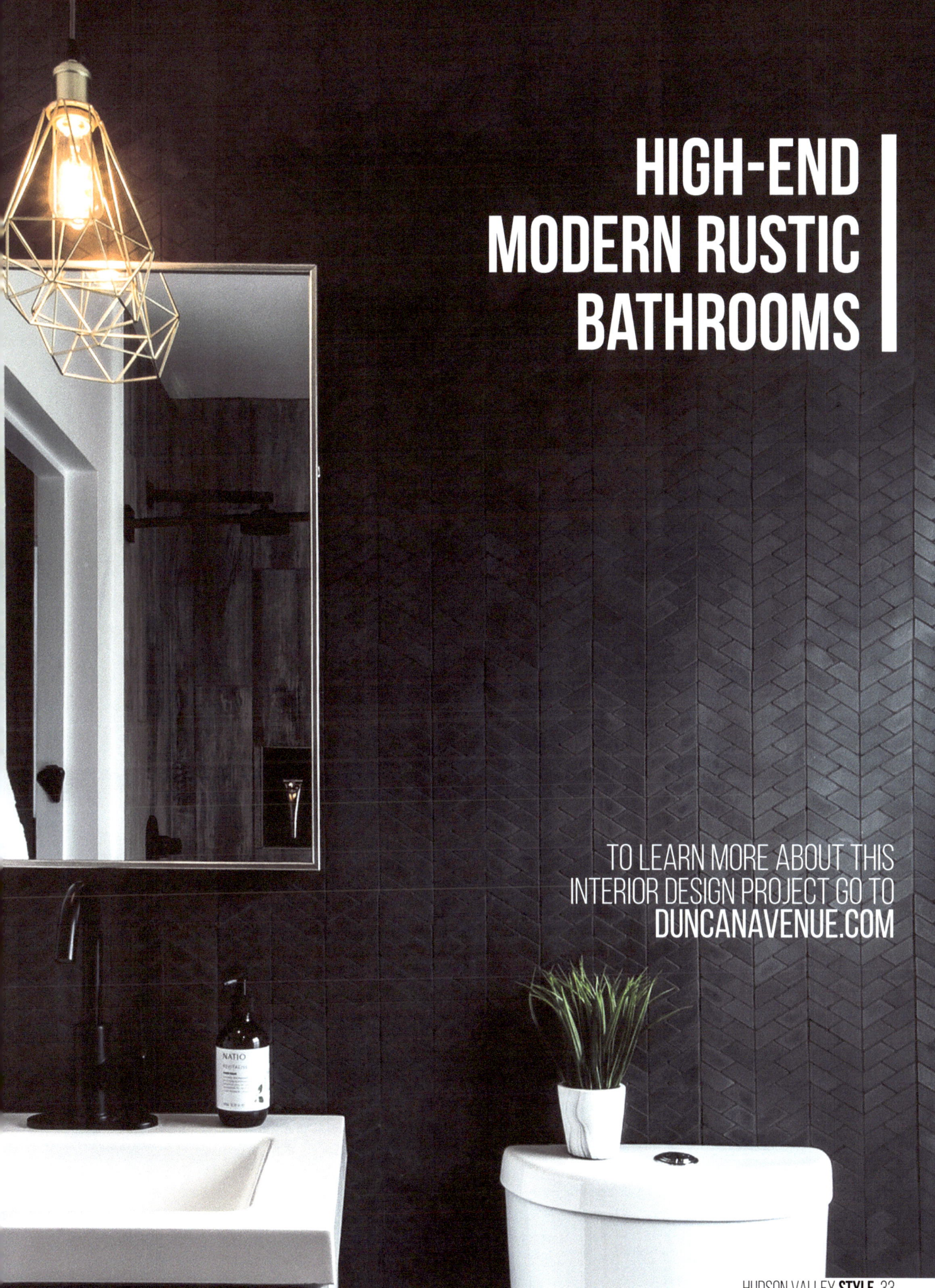

HIGH-END MODERN RUSTIC BATHROOMS

TO LEARN MORE ABOUT THIS INTERIOR DESIGN PROJECT GO TO
DUNCANAVENUE.COM

FALL 2020 COVER STORY
[KINGSTON, NY]

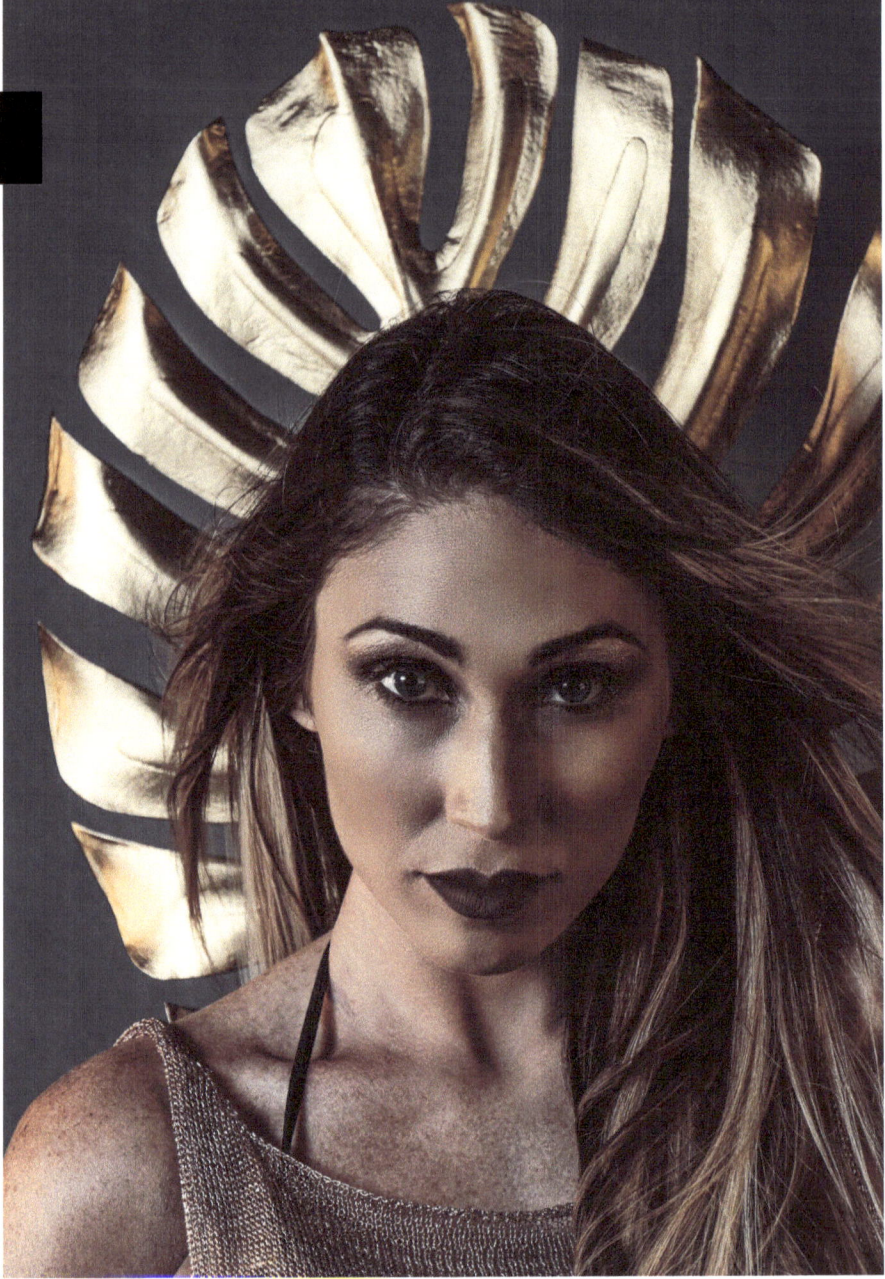

FALL 2020 COVER STORY: HUDSON VALLEY'S OWN STYLE AND BEAUTY EXPERT/REALTOR MIRANDA WEINBERGER

PHOTOGRAPHY BY MAXWELL ALEXANDER

Maxwell: Wow! we are so fortunate to have you on the cover of the Fall 2020 issue, Miranda! Amazing photoshoot and what an inspiring story we are about to share with our readers! So tell us about yourself! What is your story?

Miranda: Thank you! It is an absolute honor to be the cover feature of the Fall 2020 Issue!

I was born and raised in Kingston, New York. I graduated from Kingston High School in 2006 and immediately obtained my Cosmetology license. From there, I began working alongside my Mother in her nail salon. Over the year's I nurtured a true passion for making people look and feel their best and in 2018, I established Beauty Marc's Appearance Enhancement Studio just off of thruway exit 19, in Kingston.

Maxwell: Awesome! Kingston is amazing, I have a lot of great memories for just a year of living there. Pumpkins are so groundbreaking for the fall season :), but as a beauty expert, what do you see is trending this fall in the Hudson Valley?

Miranda: Fall in the Hudson Valley never disappoints me, but this year is exceptionally breathtaking. I see this season's trends and to me, they are looking like the 'softer side of drama'... Think of those warm metallics and mauves for Fall. Stay on-trend and trade that highlight for a rosy cheek and a nude or muted lip color.

Maxwell: Fascinating! It's almost like we always are looking for harmony with nature, even when it comes to selecting makeup colors! We happen to live in one of the most picturesque regions of the United States with all the inspiring nature around and the vibrant culture and diverse community. What is your favorite part of living in the Hudson Valley?

Miranda: My favorite thing about the Hudson Valley is hands down that picturesque landscape. The Mountains that envelope the Hudson River will never be hard to look at. I love being surrounded by orchards and wineries. There is something about the country feel of fall in the Hudson Valley that provides me with so much comfort.

Maxwell: I can definitely relate to like 100% of that :) Being an "immigrant" from NYC myself, I found Hudson Valley a very compelling contender to the city living.

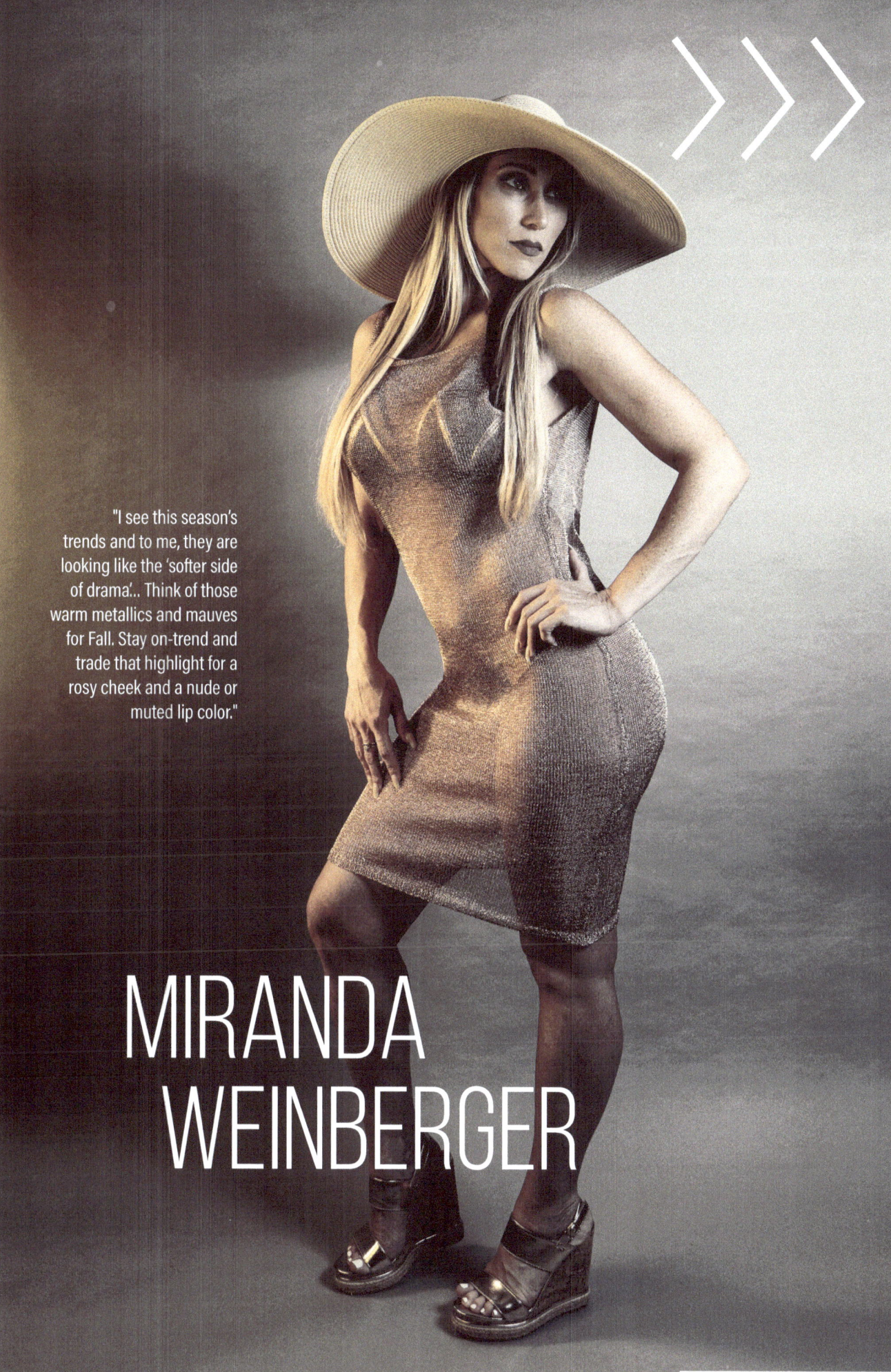

"I see this season's trends and to me, they are looking like the 'softer side of drama.'... Think of those warm metallics and mauves for Fall. Stay on-trend and trade that highlight for a rosy cheek and a nude or muted lip color."

MIRANDA WEINBERGER

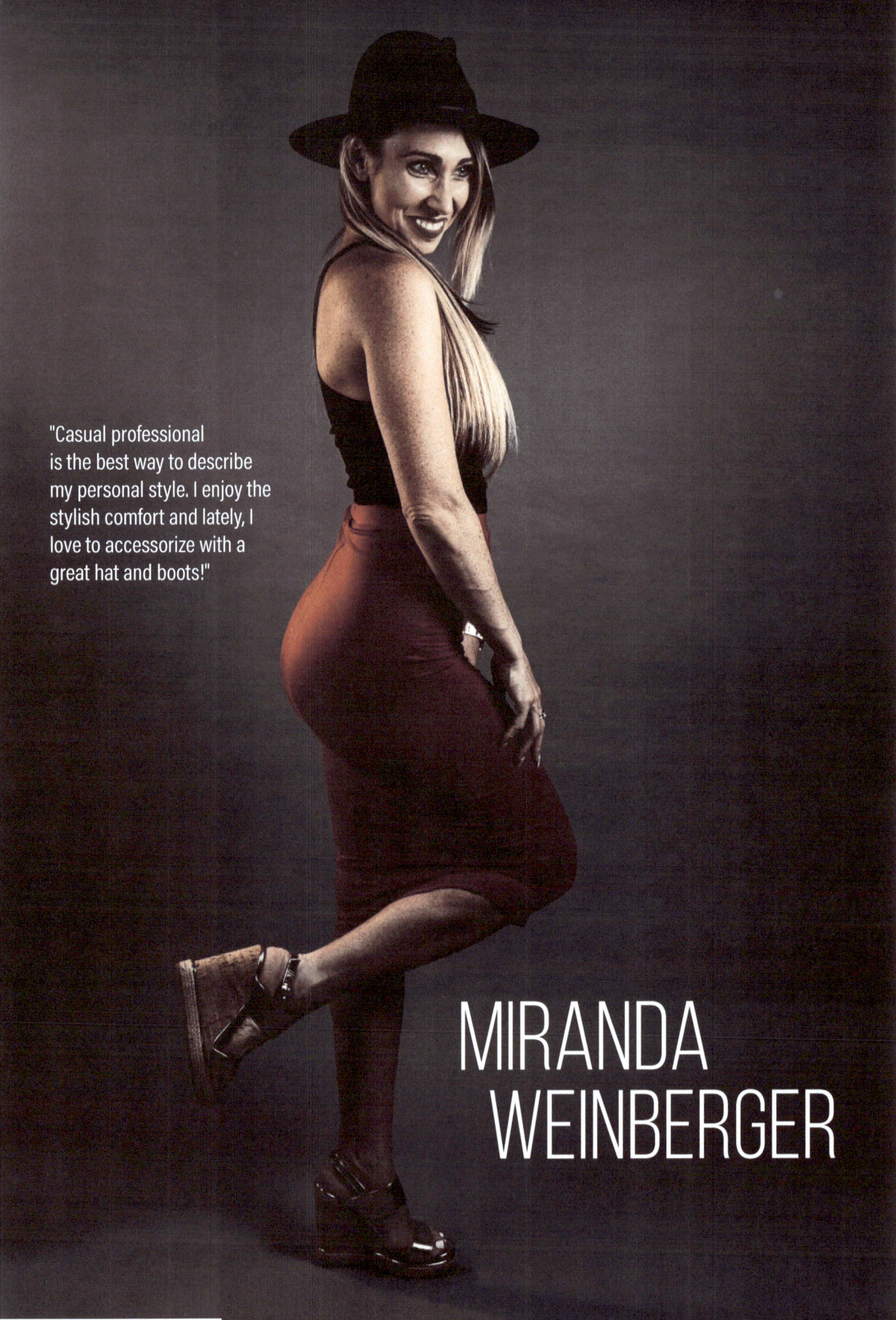

FALL 2020 COVER STORY
[KINGSTON, NY]

What about the STYLE, Hudson Valley Style to be exact. What is your definition of the term?

Miranda: Style is when various distinctions come together to form a unique whole. A notably welcome escape, I think the 'laid back' style of the Hudson Valley is palpable as so many continue to trade their fast-paced city life for the tranquil atmosphere found right here in the place I call home.

Maxwell: Sounds great! What about your own personal style?

Miranda: Casual professional is the best way to describe my personal style. I enjoy the stylish comfort and lately, I love to accessorize with a great hat and boots!

Maxwell: I heard that on top of being a model, a beauty professional, and a busy boy mom of 3, you are also one of the best

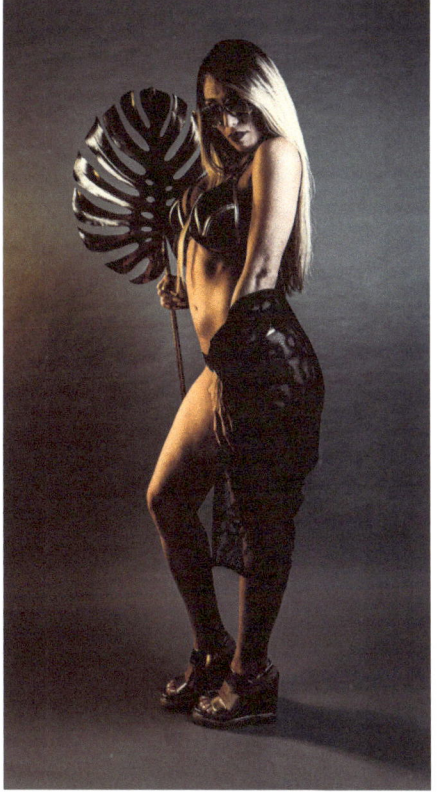

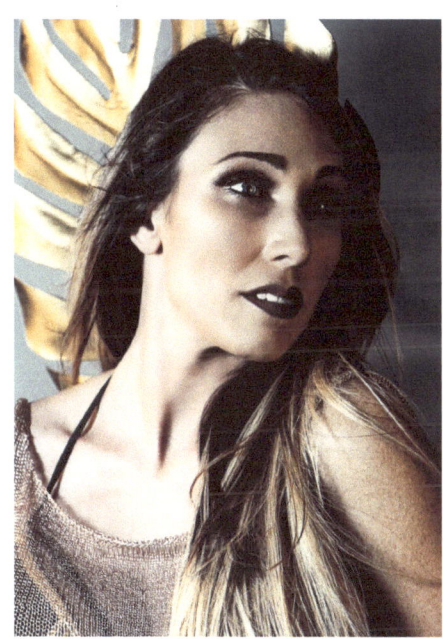

Realtors in the Hudson Valley. How had that came along and as a Realtor, what would you say to all those who are still deciding to pull the plug on their closet-sized NYC apartments and improve their lifestyle by making the move to Hudson Valley?

Miranda: For the last 13 years, being a Mom has been my main focus. As a beauty professional, the work has and will always be a passion of mine. Having the ability to make my own schedule so I can be present with my children is paramount for me. With that said, Last year I had the opportunity to pursue a career in real estate and I decided without hesitation to take the leap. I love that I can manage Motherhood, work at my salon, and also begin a journey as a Hudson Valley Realtor! I think I jumped in at the most perfect time and I can say to anyone contemplating the shift from NYC to Upstate living, there has never been a better time to explore all the Hudson Valley has to offer!

Maxwell: Well, as a millennial I am right here with you on that :) So with all that what is the next big thing for you?

Miranda: I am thrilled about my next big thing as I am starting my work as a contributing editor in the style and fashion category here at the Hudson Valley Style Magazine. Fashion has been a huge part of my life and I am excited to explore and share Hudson Valley fashion with the rest of the world.

Maxwell: Thank you so much for shedding the light on your story and I am so looking forward to circling back with you on some of the topics we discussed today and our readers are thrilled about all those style and fashion features that are coming their way directly from you!

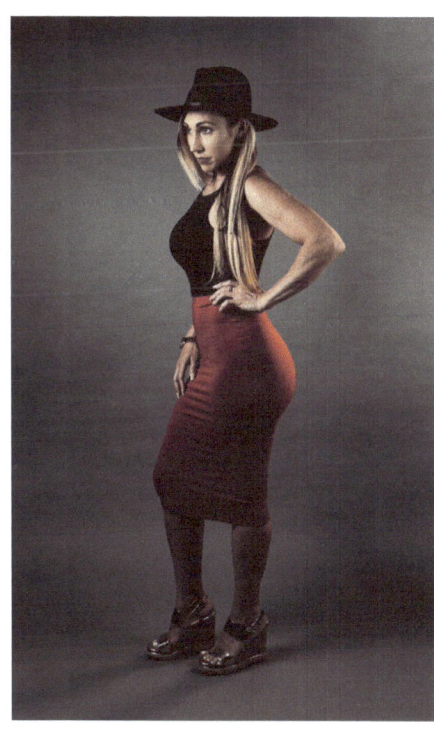

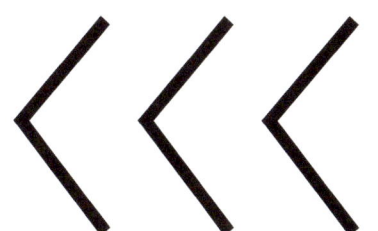

WHO IS YOUR BUYER?

[MILLENNIALS]

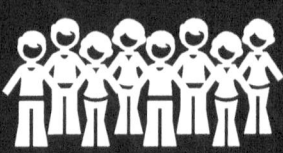 **36%** [THE LARGEST MARKET SHARE]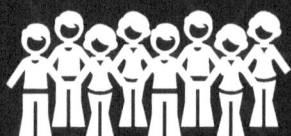

 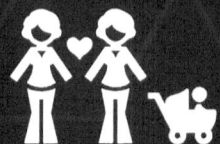 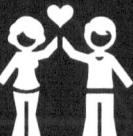

65%	48%	66%	15%
FIRST-TIME HOME BUYERS	HAVE CHILDREN	MARRIED COUPLES	UNMARRIED COUPLES

GENERATION X 38 - 52 Y/O

26% [OF ALL HOMEBUYERS]

$104,700 [MEDIAN INCOME]

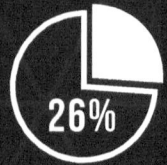

MOST LIKELY TO BE MARRIED & MOST LIKELY TO HAVE CHILDREN

[MOST RACIALLY & ETHNICALLY DIVERSE]

26% IDENTIFYING THEY ARE A RACE OTHER THAN WHITE/CAUCASIAN

 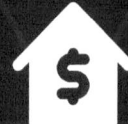

BUY THE LARGEST HOMES IN MEDIAN SQFT. | PURCHASE THE HIGHEST MEDIAN PRICED HOMES

[YOUNGER BABY BOOMERS]	[OLDER BABY BOOMERS]	[THE SILENT GENERATION]
53-62 Y/O	63-71 Y/O	72-92 Y/O
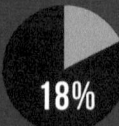 18% 	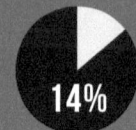 14% 	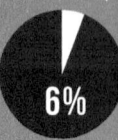 6% 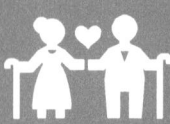

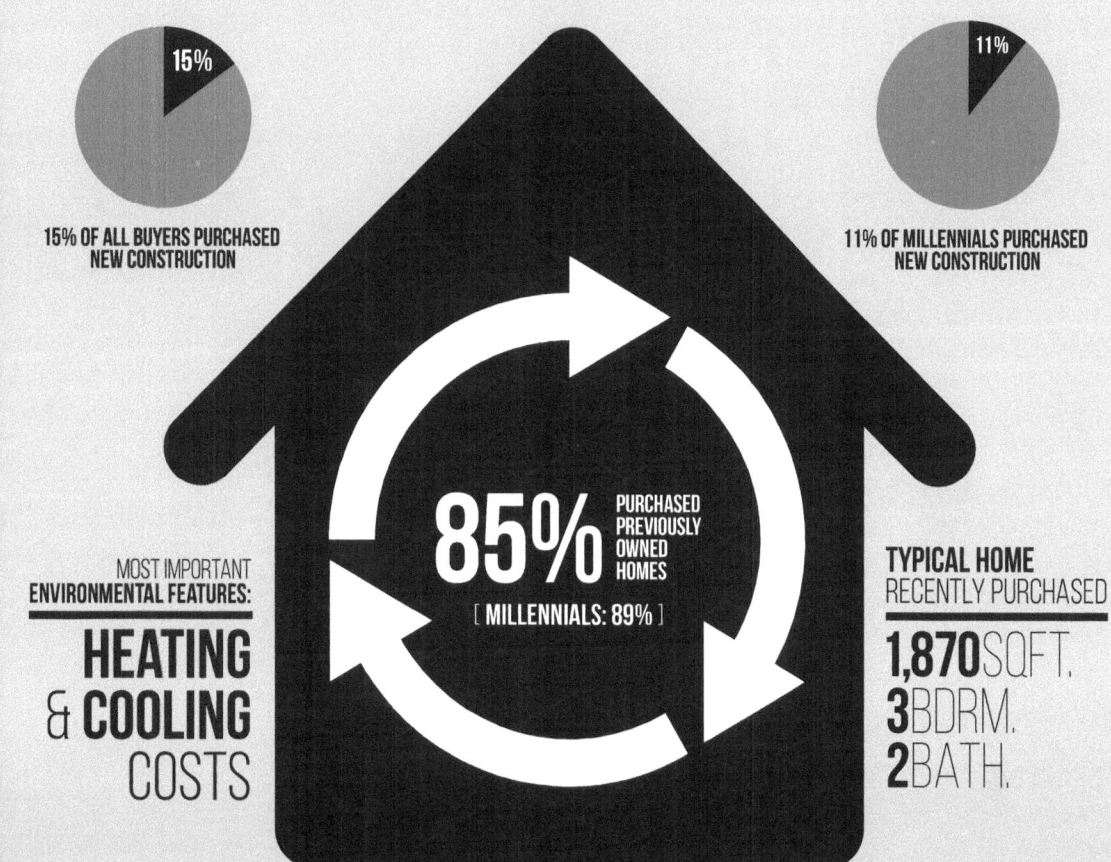

15% OF ALL BUYERS PURCHASED NEW CONSTRUCTION

11% OF MILLENNIALS PURCHASED NEW CONSTRUCTION

85% PURCHASED PREVIOUSLY OWNED HOMES
[MILLENNIALS: 89%]

MOST IMPORTANT ENVIRONMENTAL FEATURES:
HEATING & COOLING COSTS

TYPICAL HOME RECENTLY PURCHASED
1,870 SQFT.
3 BDRM.
2 BATH.

90%

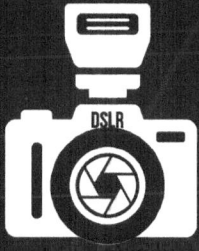

"**90% OF BUYERS** UNDER AGE OF 62 CONSIDER **PHOTOGRAPHY** AS THE MOST IMPORTANT FEATURE WHEN SEARCHING ONLINE"

DATA SOURCE: 2018 HOME BUYER AND SELLER GENERATIONAL TRENDS REPORT BY THE NATIONAL ASSOCIATION OF REALTORS®

almaxrealty ™
[ALEXANDER MAXWELL REALTY]

SELLING YOUR PROPERTY?
ASK US ABOUT **COMPLIMENTARY** ALL-INCLUSIVE
STRATEGIC MARKETING PACKAGE

LOG ON TO ALMAXREALTY.COM & JOIN US ON INSTAGRAM! @ALMAXREALTY

[PRESENTED BY ALMAXREALTY.COM]

IN THE BUSINESS OF BEAUTY

[FISHKILL, NY]

Exclusive Interview with Dr. Zainab Mogul-Ashraf (Dr. Z) of Hebe Medical Spa
Interview and Photography by Maxwell Alexander

Maxwell: Thank you for the interview opportunity and an amazing photoshoot, Dr. Z! I must say you are a natural when it comes to modeling. Great job! Please tell us a little bit about yourself and how did the idea of Hebe Medical Spa manifest in your life.

Dr. Z: Well thank you! :) We have done a few photoshoots the last couple of years and I can say I definitely feel more comfortable with it now! Not so much in the beginning.

I am an internist and I have always been interested in aesthetics, beauty, and fashion. I grew up with 3 sisters and we always played with makeup and were always interested in skincare. I also found great satisfaction in helping people feel better about their appearance and felt getting into aesthetics was a natural progression for me. I felt my training as an internist led med to look at the body as a whole and focus on wellness and beauty from the inside out. This gives me a different perspective and approach when it comes to working with my clients. About 3 years ago I met my business partner Irina in the gym. We were the only 2 women at 5 am in the morning pumping some serious iron. One day we started talking and we clicked and found so many things in common. We were both professional women, we were both into a healthy lifestyle and also believed in empowering men and women to be the best version of themselves. We formed a close friendship and one day I shared with her the idea I had to open a medical spa and I asked her if she would be interested to be my business partner and help me bring this idea to life. And the rest is history…

Maxwell: Wow! Great story and a testimony to the fact that great minds think alike! Today I'd like to talk to you about the concept of eternal beauty and what it means to you as a beauty industry expert. Looking at the beautiful masterpieces of art, like the Mona Lisa by Leonardo Da Vinci, that depicted beauty in his time, we all can see that the definition of ideal human body composition has evolved dramatically throughout the history of civilization. At the same time, we can draw some parallels that do stay current and priceless even today. What is your take on that?

Dr. Z: I believe that beauty comes from the inside out and outside in. What I mean by that is that for one to be the best version of themselves they have to feel good on the inside. They can achieve that through a wholesome diet, exercise, and daily meditation, or any other form of relaxation and self-development. There is also a lot to be said about waking up, looking in the mirror, and loving what you see. A lot of our clients come to us and one thing they say they want is to have clear skin so they don't have to wear makeup. Clear skin is youthful skin. Having flawless skin, less fine and wrinkles and feeling youthful and beautiful is such a confidence booster. This is where we come! When a person feels good about themselves, they are more motivated to do better in all areas of their lives. Our client's age ranges from the early '20s to the 80s. The young ladies in their 20s and 30s understand the importance of prevention and they start their Botox and care for their skin with facials, lasers, and good medically graded skin care products. We have a lot of clients in their 50s that come to us and their goal is to look as refreshed and youthful as possible. We can help with injectables, laser skin rejuvenation, and correction of sun damage, tone, and texture of the skin. For

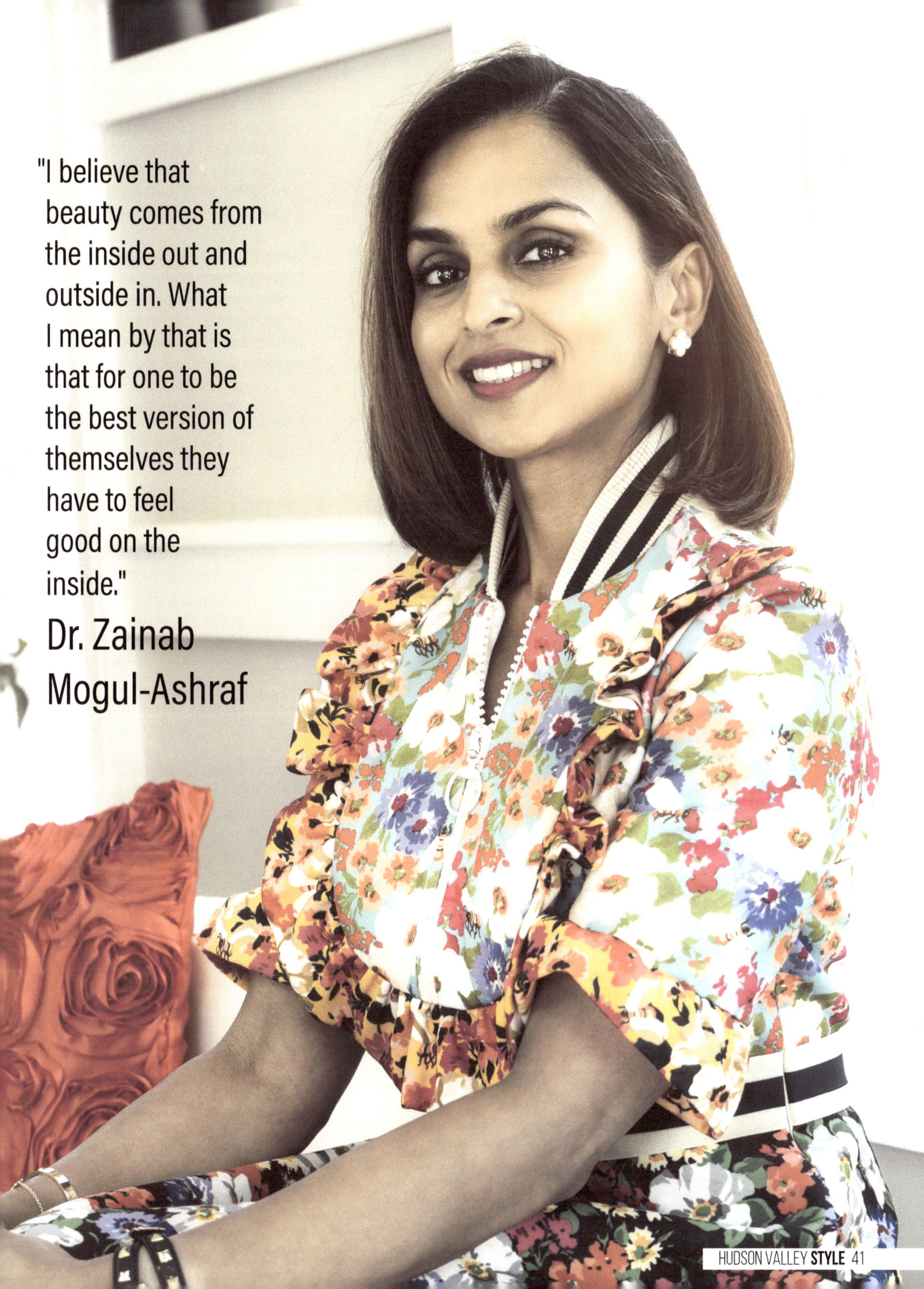

"I believe that beauty comes from the inside out and outside in. What I mean by that is that for one to be the best version of themselves they have to feel good on the inside."

Dr. Zainab Mogul-Ashraf

our ladies in their 60s and 70s, getting old is a gift, and bc we are getting old it doesn't mean we can't feel vibrant and beautiful.

Maxwell: Seems like our generation has gotten a lot closer to finding that elusive fountain of youth, I guess :) But what about some other natural beauty concepts that you come across in your line of work?

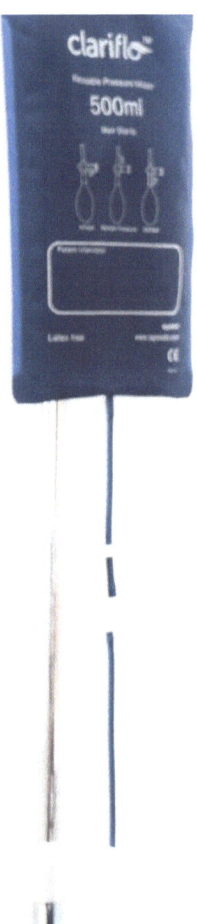

Dr. Z: Hebe Medical Spa is one of the best spas in the Hudson Valley and we offer numerous treatments from any injectable neuromodulators, dermal fillers, injectable bio stimulators, hair restoration, bioidentical hormone replacement therapy, laser skin rejuvenation, robotic micro-needling, laser hair removal, body contouring, weight loss program, IV vitamin therapy and more. When a client comes for a consultation I start with what their concerns are and figure out what treatments will be the best suited for them to help with those concerns. I always prioritize the treatments by safety first, second is downtime and last is cost. Also, I always think about not only delivering short term results for my clients but also long term effects of the treatments. I spend a lot of time and resources getting trained by the best injectors in the world and keep up with the latest injectable

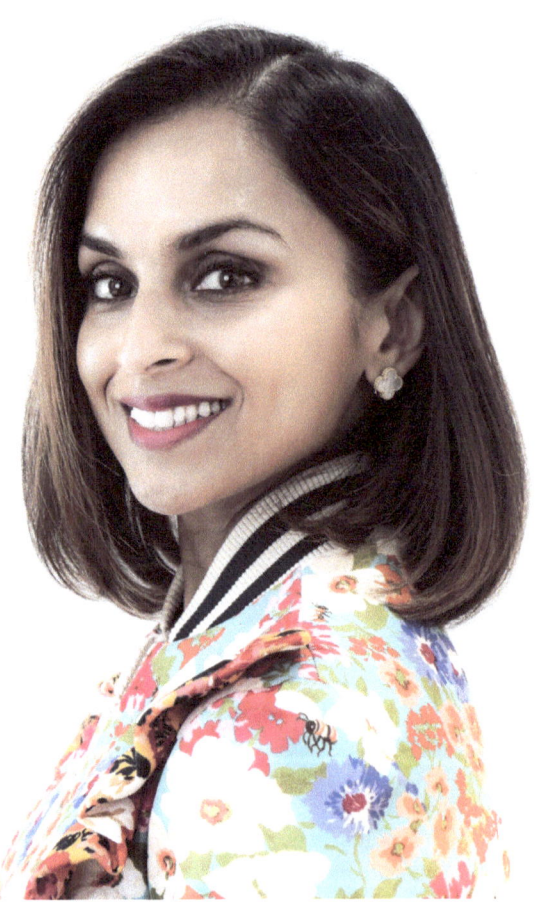

techniques because I always strive to deliver the best and most natural results for my clients.

One of the treatments that have gained tremendous interest lately is lip enhancements. I think thanks to IG and the Kardashians big luscious lips have become quite of a trend nowadays. I love doing lips, I take my time to make sure I create size and shape that enhances my client's facial structure. The smile on their faces when I am done is very gratifying. We have a sign in the spa that says " you live once, buy yourself lips" I think that sums it all.

Maxwell: Fascinating! And yes, I can relate to some of that myself, but that's going to be another story :) Talking about your clients – the general assumption is that it's the ladies who are so particular about their looks and the appearance of age, but what about the guys? What are they into when it comes to your services?

Dr. Z: You will be surprised to know but men are one of the fastest-growing patient segments in aesthetics and why shouldn't they be??? Men, just like women want to look like the best version of themselves and age gracefully. Taking care of their skin has become part of their grooming. Botox and dermal fillers for men can reduce the signs of aging. Of course, the approach to male aesthetics differs from that of females. Men have a squarer face, a more angled and larger jaw, and equally balanced upper and lower facial proportions. Facial muscle mass, subcutaneous tissue, and blood vessel density are also increased in men relative to women. So the techniques and amount of injectables I use are different for men and women. Men are great candidates for laser skin rejuvenation, laser hair removal, IV vitamin therapy, hair restoration, and bio-identical hormone replacement therapy. We also do regular facials. So if someone has no experience and is not sure where to start a facial membership is a great start and build from there.

Maxwell: I'm on it, Dr. Z! Now I know that it's never too early to start on my Botox shots :) When is your next Botox party? ... Anyways, in an interview a couple of years ago Hebe Med Spa had a goal of bringing all the state of the art beauty treatments to its clients in Fishkill, New York, today your clients are coming not only from all over the Hudson Valley, but all the way from New York City and even from across the country! What happened here?

Dr. Z: You got it right! One of the things I am very proud of is the reputation we have developed as skin and beauty experts in the area and I think a good reputation travels very fast nowadays. Hebe Med Spa has established itself as an expert in medical-grade beauty treatments and thanks to our big following and overwhelming support from social media we see more and more clients from beyond the Hudson Valley region. We also get tons of client referrals, which to us is the biggest compliment we can get and we truly appreciate the support! We have a big range of treatments form the state of the art equipment for skin rejuvenation, body contouring, robotic micro-needling, laser hair removal, bio-identical hormone replacement therapy, IV Vitamins, hair restoration, ample assortment of dermal fillers, Botox, collagen-stimulating injectables, PDO threads for non-surgical facelifts using the latest and most advanced techniques to create beautiful and natural results. We also have facial and laser memberships that

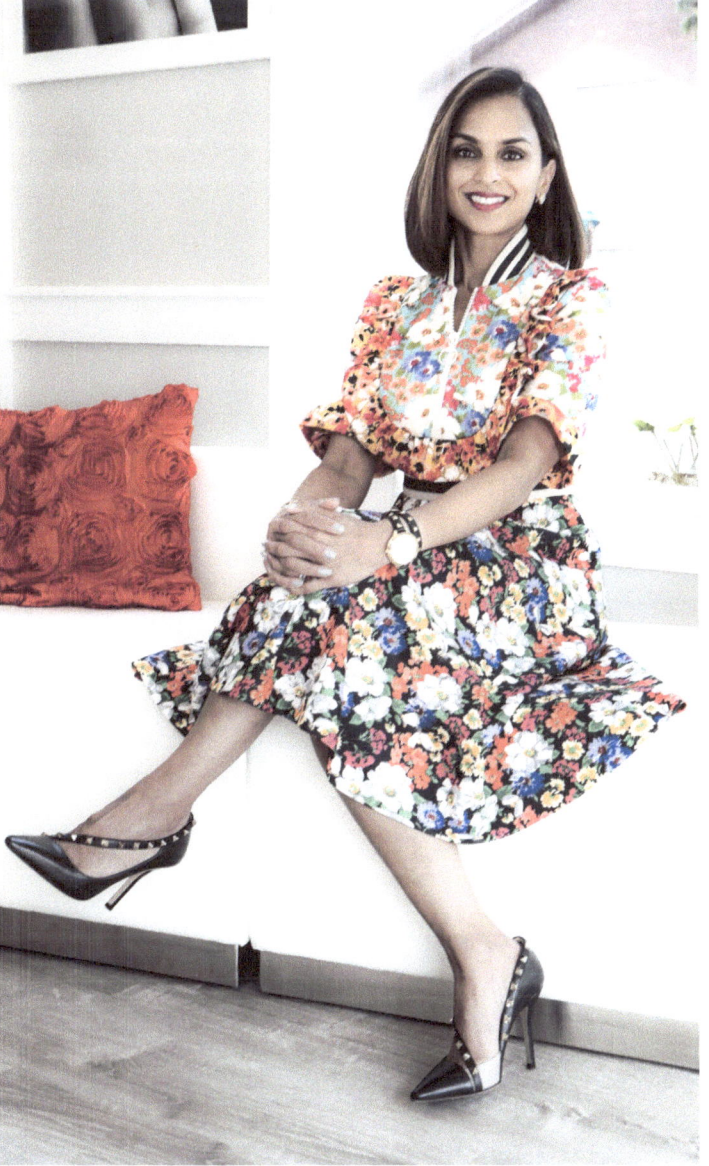

are very affordable and make achieving and maintaining beautiful skin accessible to everyone. This month we are also launching Botox and filler membership and we are very excited about it. Taking care of your skin and staying fresh and youthful should be a part of your grooming and the memberships make that available to a lot more people.

Maxwell: Just wow! And the way to go! So what's next? What new beauty treatments should we discuss in our next sit down?

Dr. Z: As you know we are committed to always bringing the best, most advanced, non-invasive devices and procedures that deliver amazing results in the safest way possible. Here at Hebe, the best medical spa in Hudson Valley, our ethos is clear skin is youthful skin! No matter how much filler and Botox we inject in your face if your skin is not up to par you will never be completely satisfied with your results. But if you get your sun damage and pigmentation cleared, shrink the size of your pores, improve the tone and texture of your skin and minimize your fine lines and wrinkles that will make a permanent improvement. And this is where the lasers come in very handy. We have different devices that address different skin concerns. For example, our newest device is a skin resurfacing laser that resurfaces the top layer of the skin, it's a beautiful treatment for fine lines and wrinkles, moderate sun damage, tone, and texture of the skin. The results are amazing and it is minimal downtime. We just introduced PDO Threads for facelift and collagen building. We are the only provider in the area that offers the PDO threads. We also have a Botox and filler membership that we are introducing in the month of October that will allow our clients to stay on schedule with their treatments without breaking the bank. I think the culture is changing the services we offer are no longer a luxury, they are becoming part of our grooming. We love what we do and we love our clients! We have created a beautiful environment for our clients and we have an amazing team! Please, come and let us be the one helping you with your pro-aging journey to become the best version of yourself.

Maxwell: Thank you so much, Dr. Z and I can't wait for our next story about the laser skincare treatments, it feels like the future is already here :)

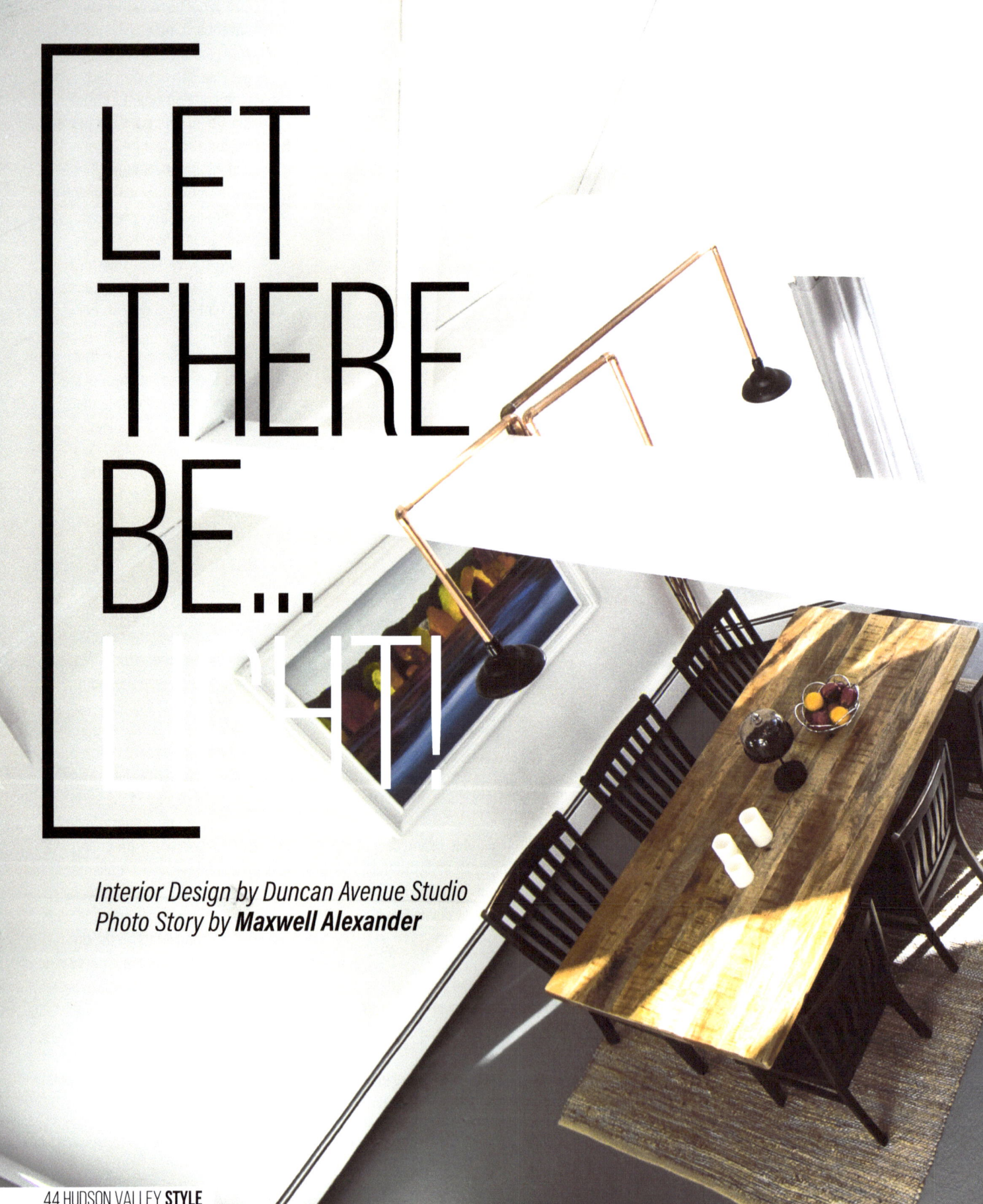

[HUDSON VALLEY STYLE LIVING]

[LET THERE BE... LIGHT!

Interior Design by Duncan Avenue Studio
Photo Story by **Maxwell Alexander**

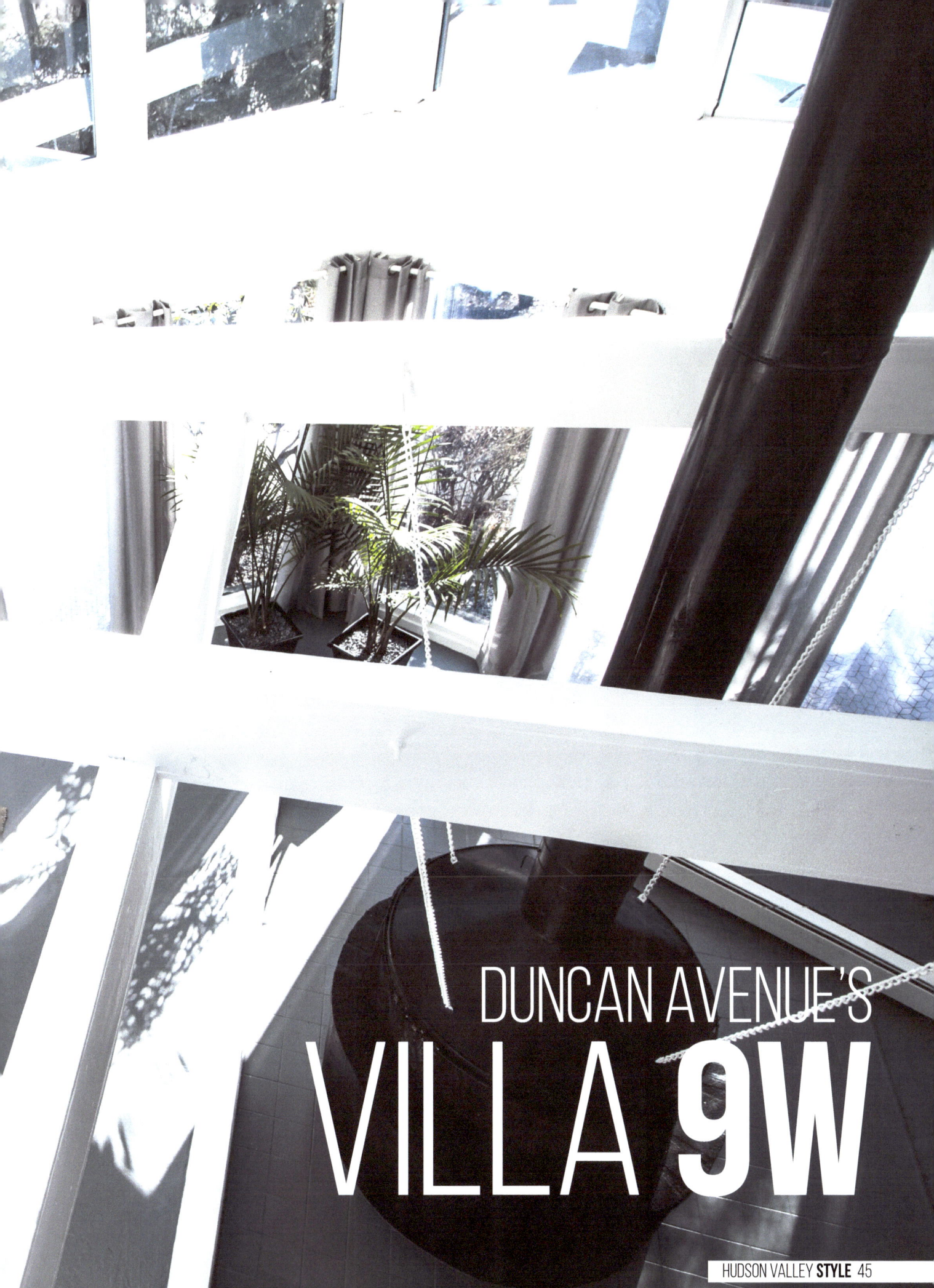

DUNCAN AVENUE'S VILLA 9W

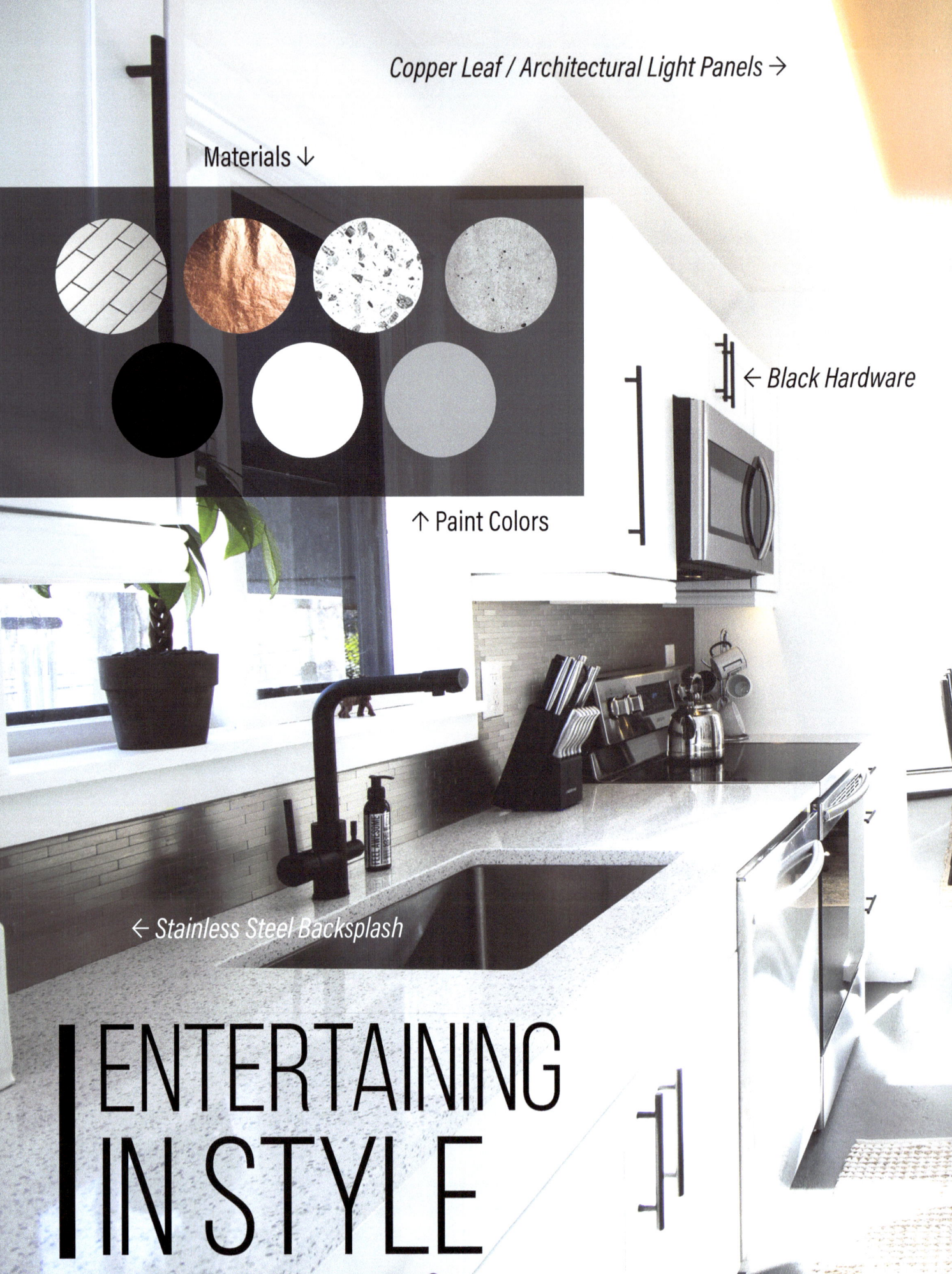

ENTERTAINING IN STYLE

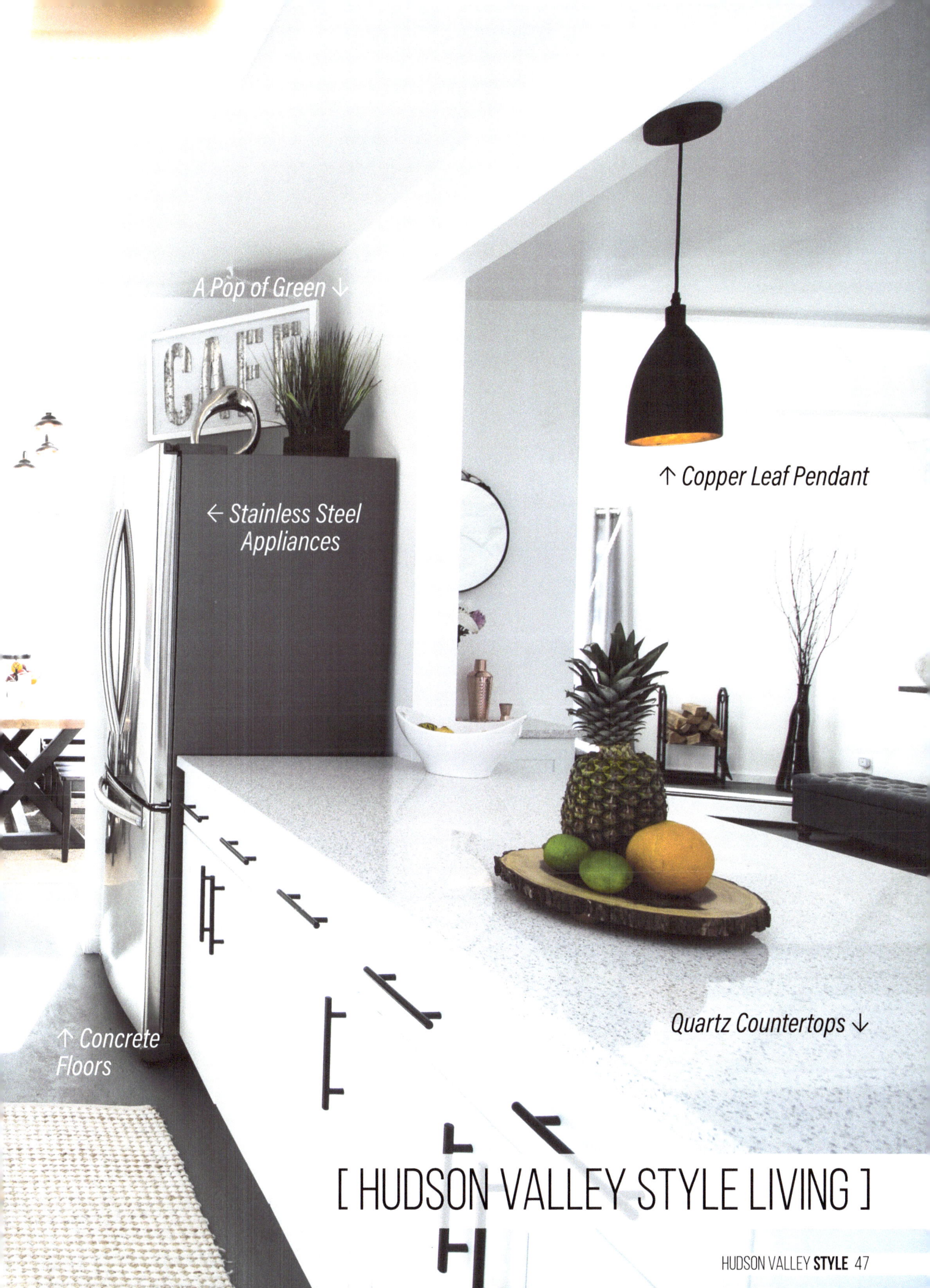

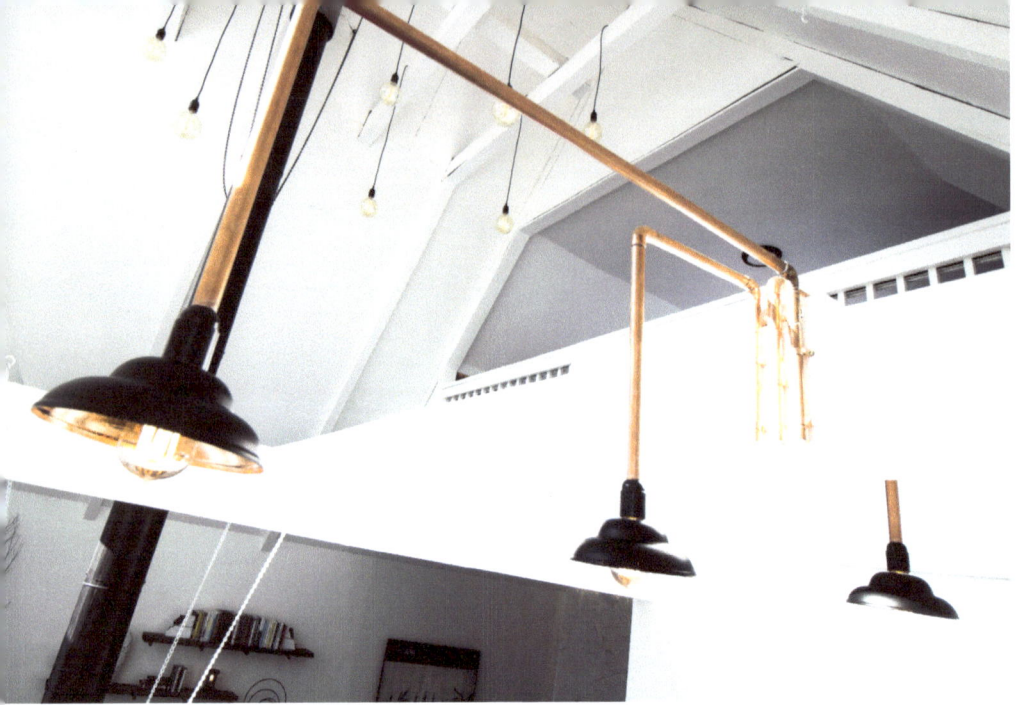

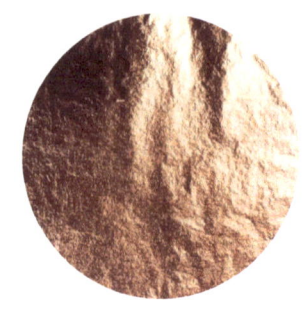

← *Custom Copper Lights*
© Duncan Avenue Design

White Granite Wall →

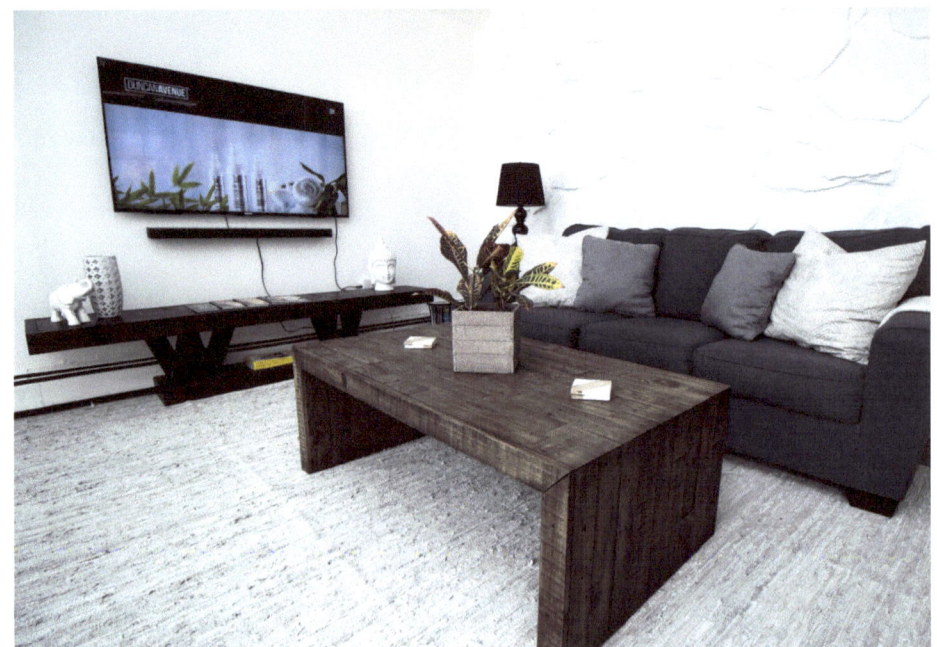

Wood Accents →

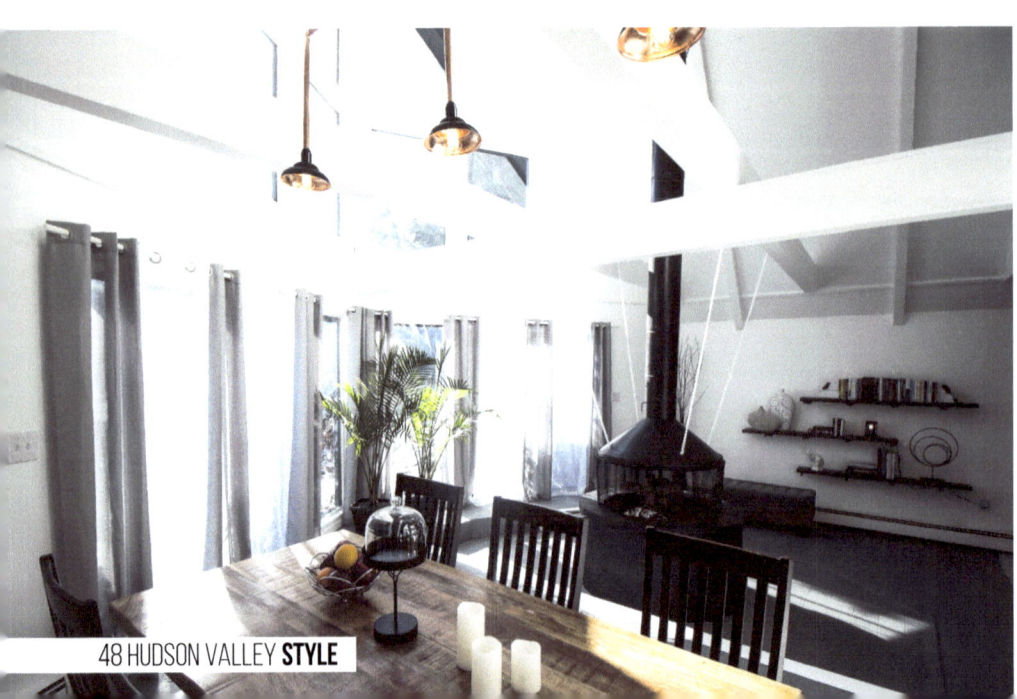

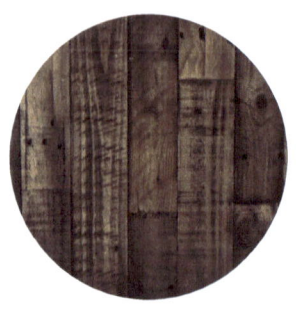

← *Formal Dining Area*

LIVING | WHITE
SPACE | BALANCE

Custom Entertainment
↓ *Console*

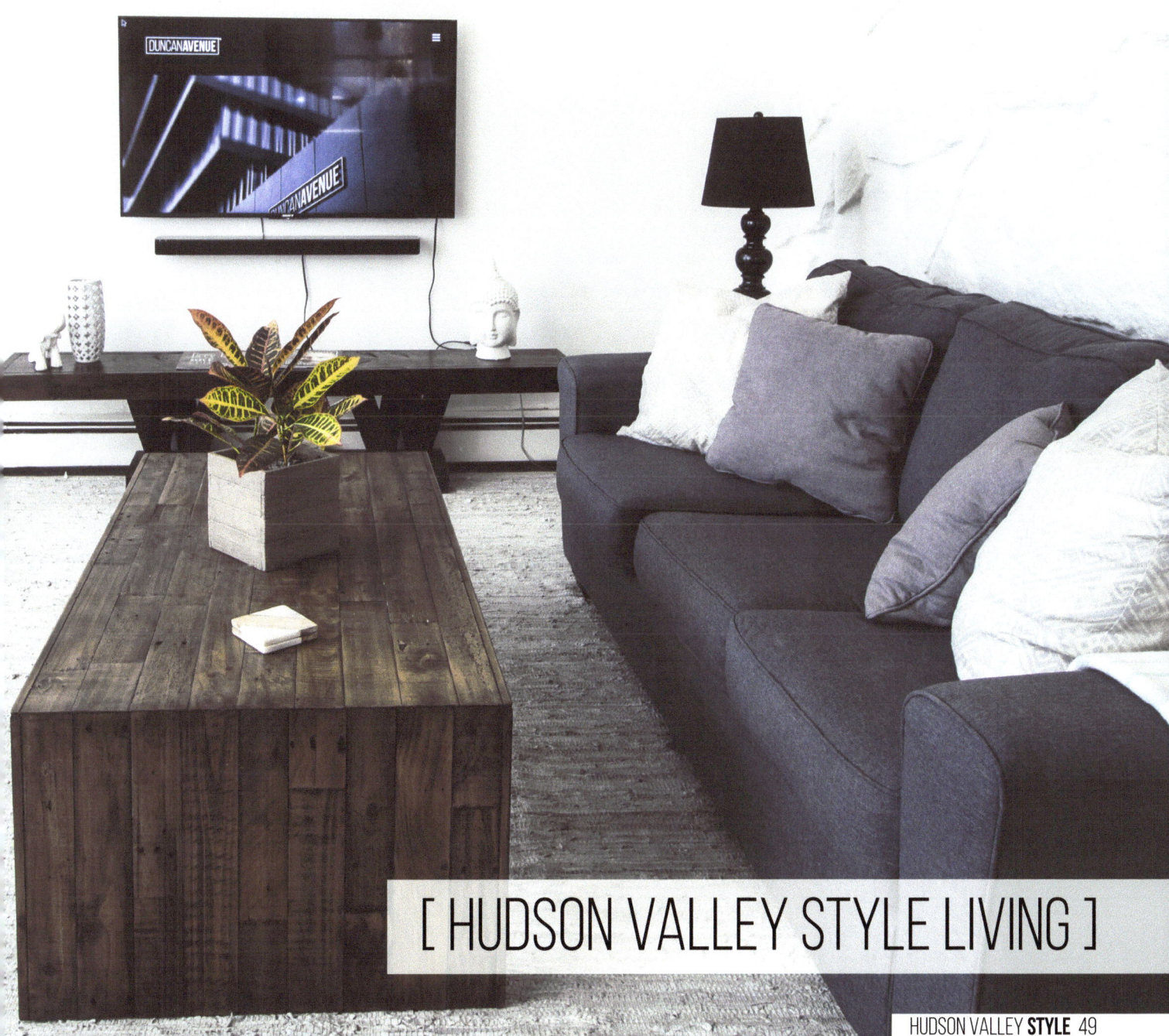

[HUDSON VALLEY STYLE LIVING]

REAL ESTATE PHOTOGRAPHY 101

61% MORE VIEWS ONLINE WITH PROFESSIONAL PHOTOS

UP TO **47%** HIGHER ASKING PRICE/SQFT

80% OF BUYERS CITED THEY WOULDN'T EVEN CONSIDER A LISTING WITHOUT PHOTOGRAPHS

98% OF BUYERS THINK PROFESSIONAL PHOTOS ARE MOST USEFUL WHEN LOOKING FOR HOME ONLINE

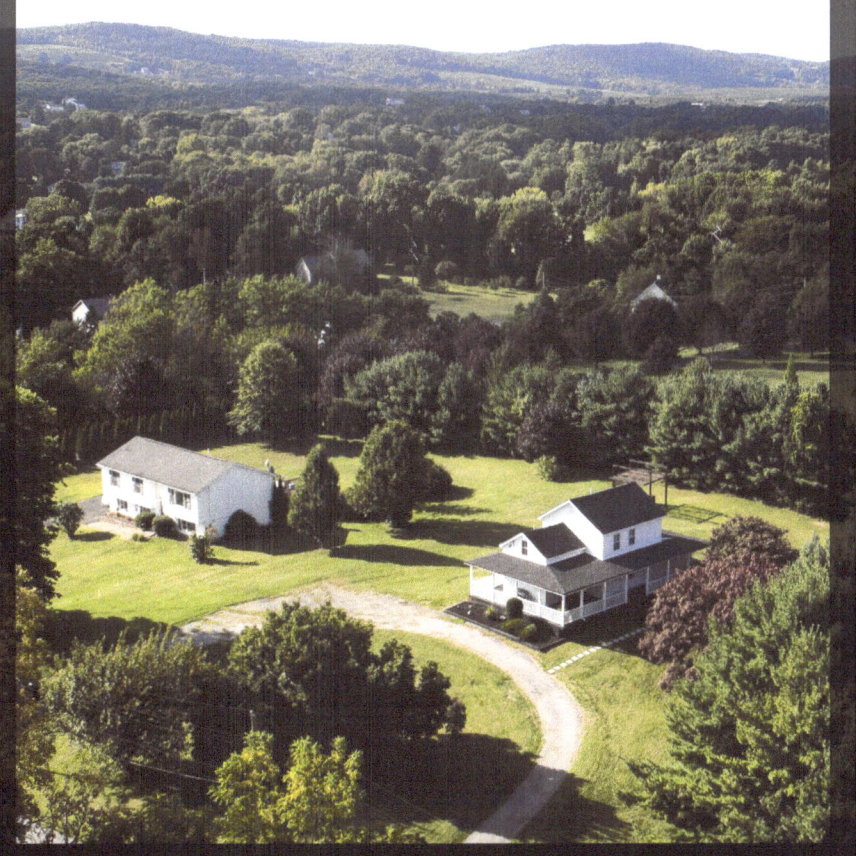
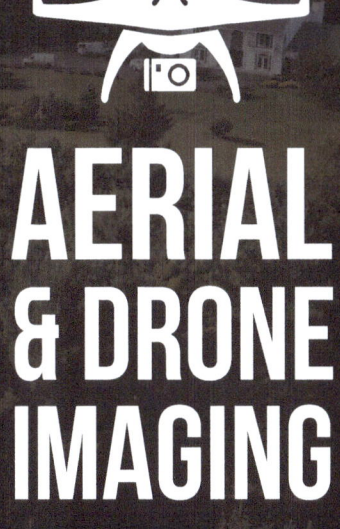

AERIAL & DRONE IMAGING

CONSIDER THESE HIGH-TECH UPGRADES

DUNCAN AVENUE
HUDSON VALLEY REAL ESTATE SERVICES

SCHEDULE YOUR PHOTOSHOOT @
DUNCANAVENUE.COM

STATISTICS SOURCE:
NATIONAL ASSOCIATION OF REALTORS

PROFESSIONAL LIGHTING
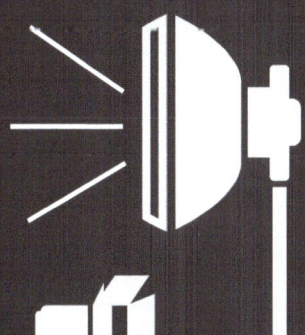

DSLR CAMERAS & LENSES
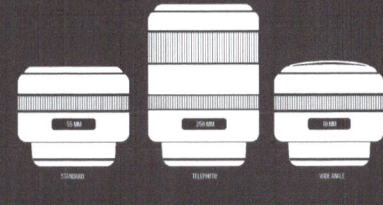
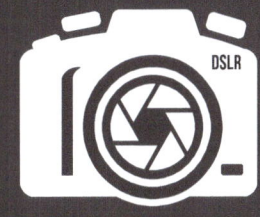

PROFESSIONAL RETOUCHING

+ DIGITAL STAGING
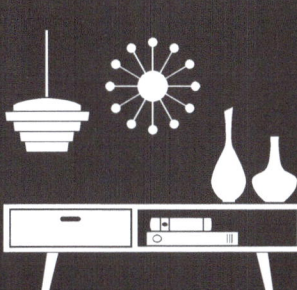

The way people buy and sell things has inherently changed in the last decade. Why should real estate be any different? The industry as you know it is lagging dreadfully behind, but Almax Realty is disrupting the system with a bold, new outlook on what is necessary to become a successful real estate agent.

CUTTING-EDGE ENVIRONMENT

Contrary to the notion that we're all lazy and entitled, Millennials are overtaking the workforce and the real estate market. Alexander Maxwell Realty understands your need for a cutting-edge environment to thrive in. We're not talking about gimmicks like bean bags and espresso bars; we are talking about a technology-powered system designed for agents that operate differently—a system that enables you to succeed.

THE OPPORTUNITY IS IN THE FIELD

As a matter of fact, the less you see our office, the better, even though it's a beautiful office. We do not require you to waste time on senseless, hierarchical office duties because the opportunity is in the field. You get what you put in, and with a flexible schedule that allows you to work as much or as little as you'd like, not a minute is wasted. Our agency is not the old boy's club that you know so well. We think of ourselves as business partners, providing you with all the tools it takes to go from showing to closing, to an unrivaled commission check in your bank account.

WORLD-CLASS MARKETING

At Almax Realty, our agents are always moving forward. Our commission structure is based on a true buyer's agent 90-10 split, with no extra charges or fees. We are not in the business of thievery. We strive to invest in our agents from day one by providing honest commission for honest work, and an arsenal of world-class marketing materials to help you build strong client relationships. From complimentary, strategic marketing packages to award-winning photography, we have your back.

CONTROL YOUR DESTINY

Alexander Maxwell Realty is a platform where you control your destiny and your career, and we want to do everything we can to help you reach your goals. Support and innovation are the pillars on which that platform lies, and our core values transcend the hollow text on a mission statement. We have a growing team of highly motivated, like-minded agents and we are always looking for more, so just drop us a line to get started!

LEARN MORE & APPLY TO JOIN AT ALMAXREALTY.COM

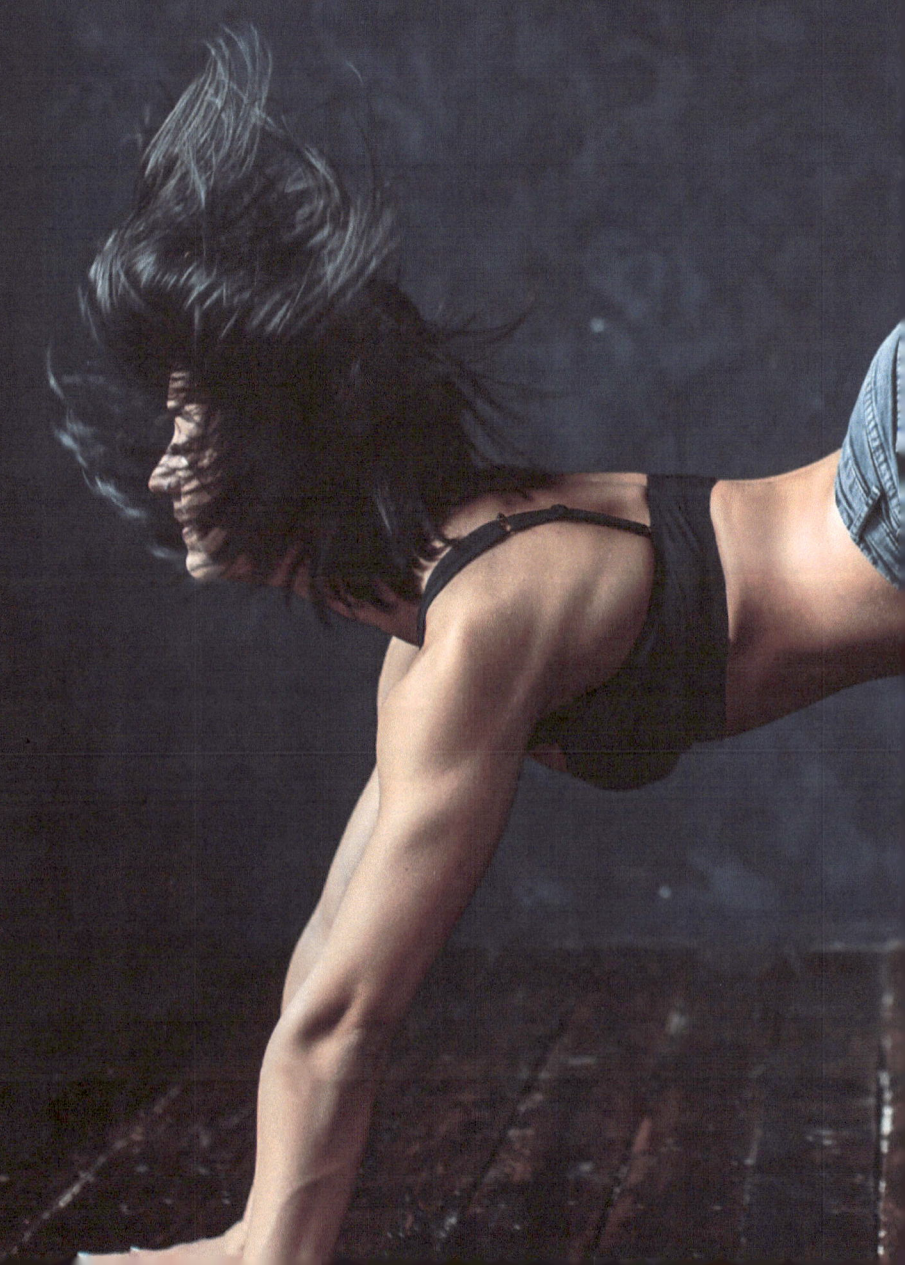

#FRESH
#AMBITIOUS
#VICTORIOUS
#JOINUS

[REAL ESTATE STYLE]

JOIN HUDSON VALLEY'S BEST REAL ESTATE AGENCY

BY DINO ALEXANDER
CEO, ALEXANDER MAXWELL REALTY

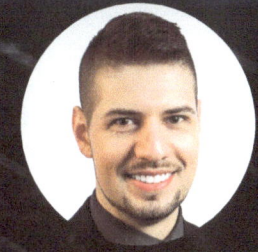

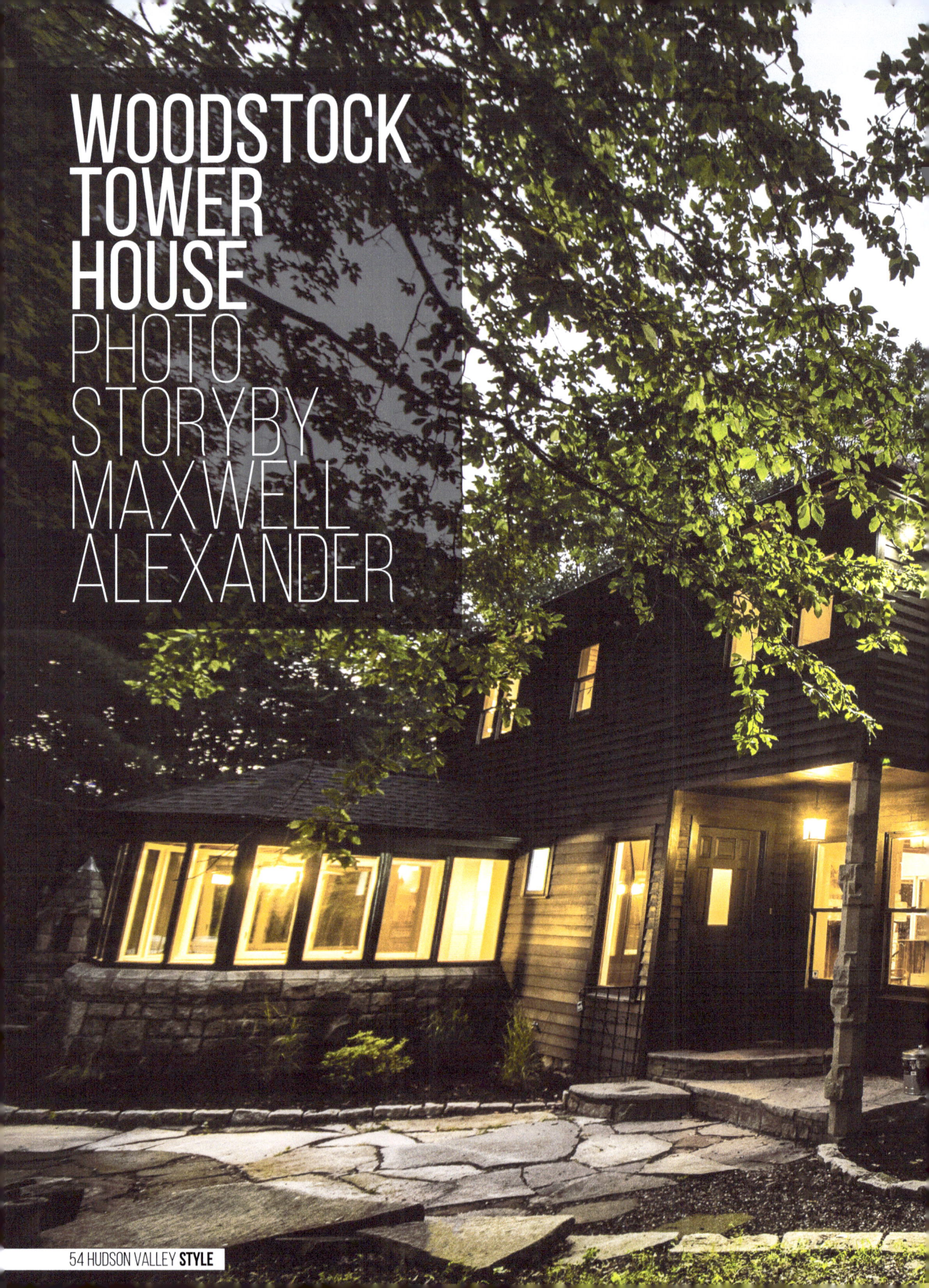

WOODSTOCK TOWER HOUSE
PHOTO STORY BY MAXWELL ALEXANDER

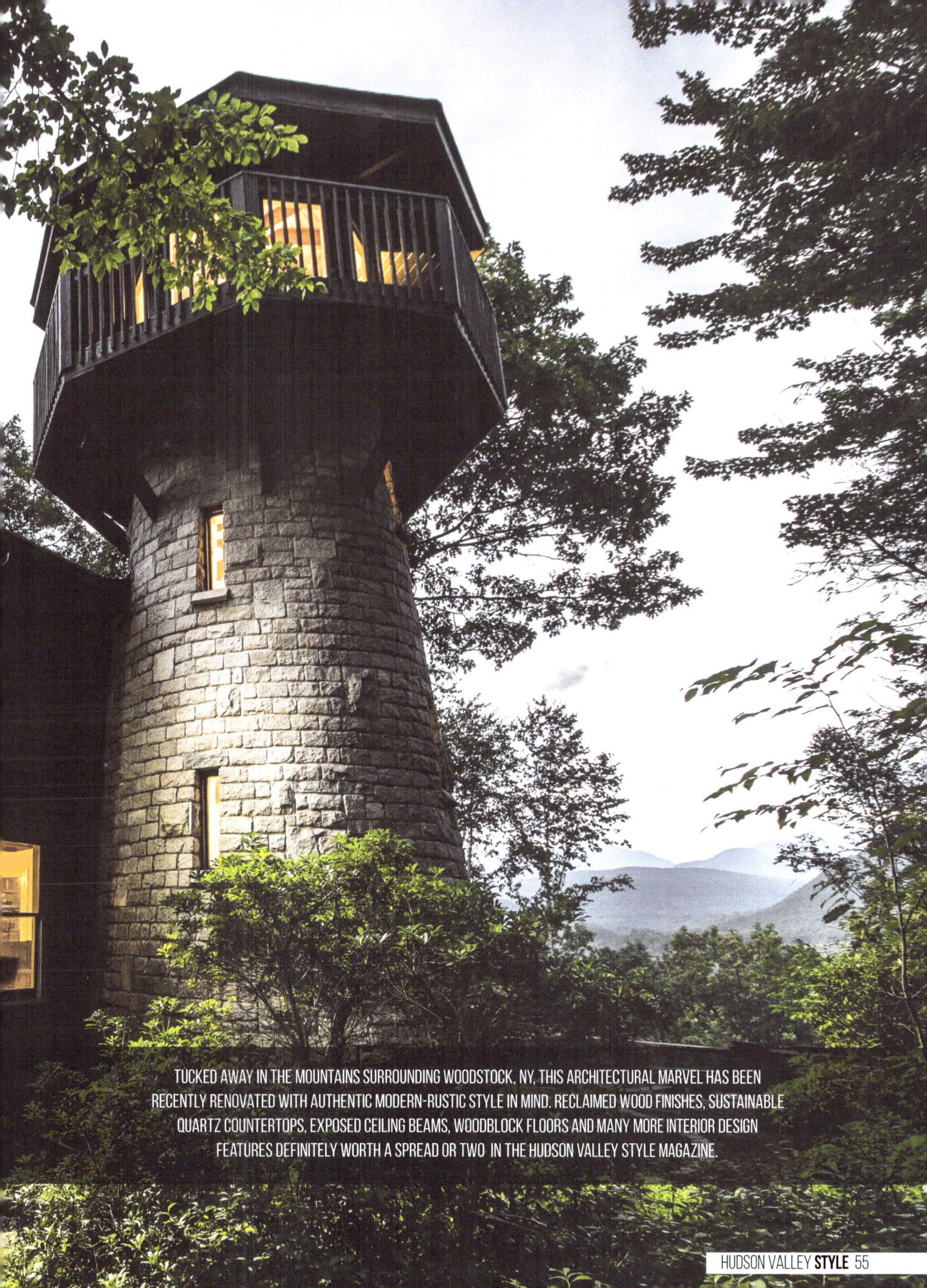

TUCKED AWAY IN THE MOUNTAINS SURROUNDING WOODSTOCK, NY, THIS ARCHITECTURAL MARVEL HAS BEEN RECENTLY RENOVATED WITH AUTHENTIC MODERN-RUSTIC STYLE IN MIND. RECLAIMED WOOD FINISHES, SUSTAINABLE QUARTZ COUNTERTOPS, EXPOSED CEILING BEAMS, WOODBLOCK FLOORS AND MANY MORE INTERIOR DESIGN FEATURES DEFINITELY WORTH A SPREAD OR TWO IN THE HUDSON VALLEY STYLE MAGAZINE.

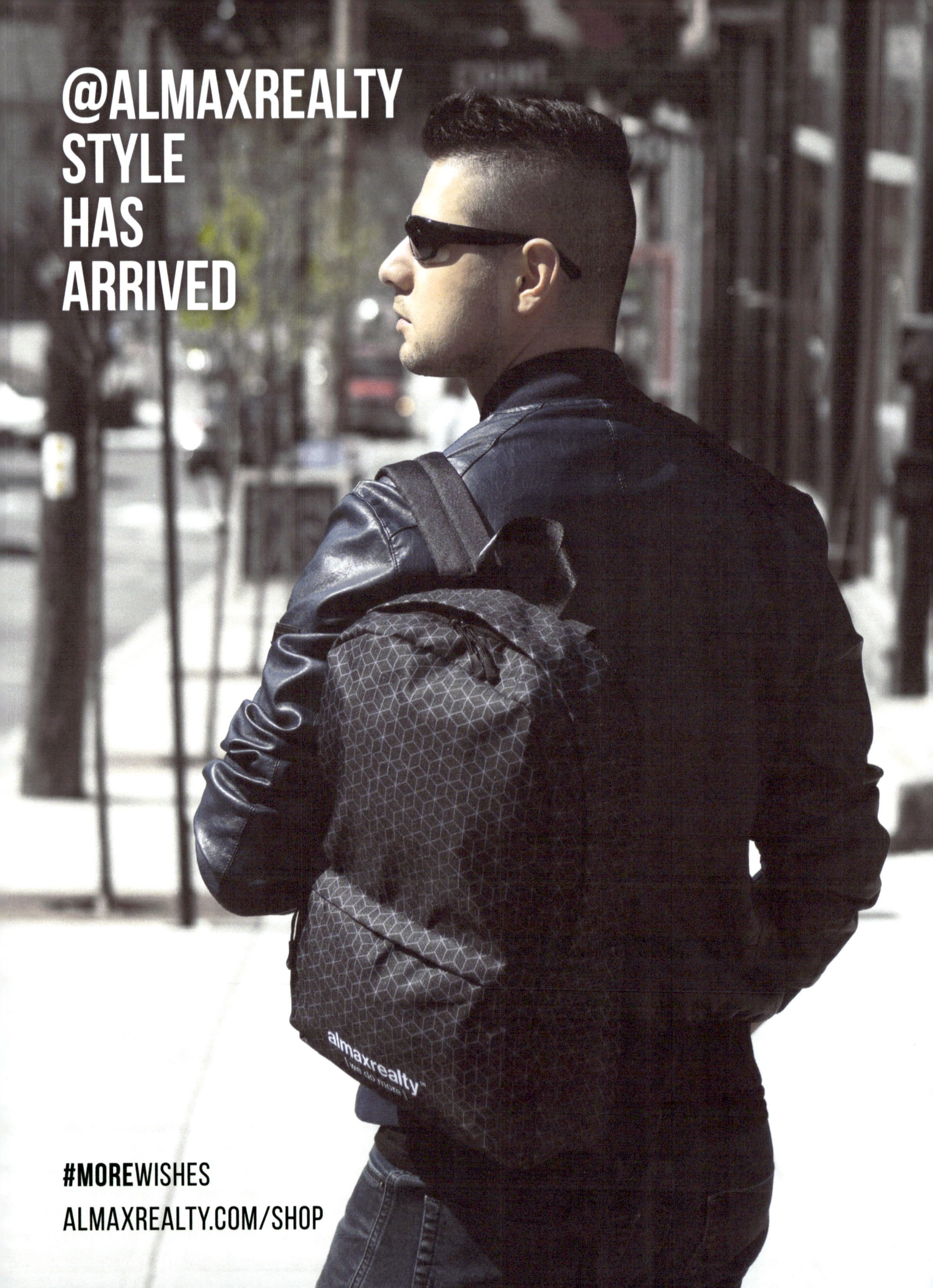

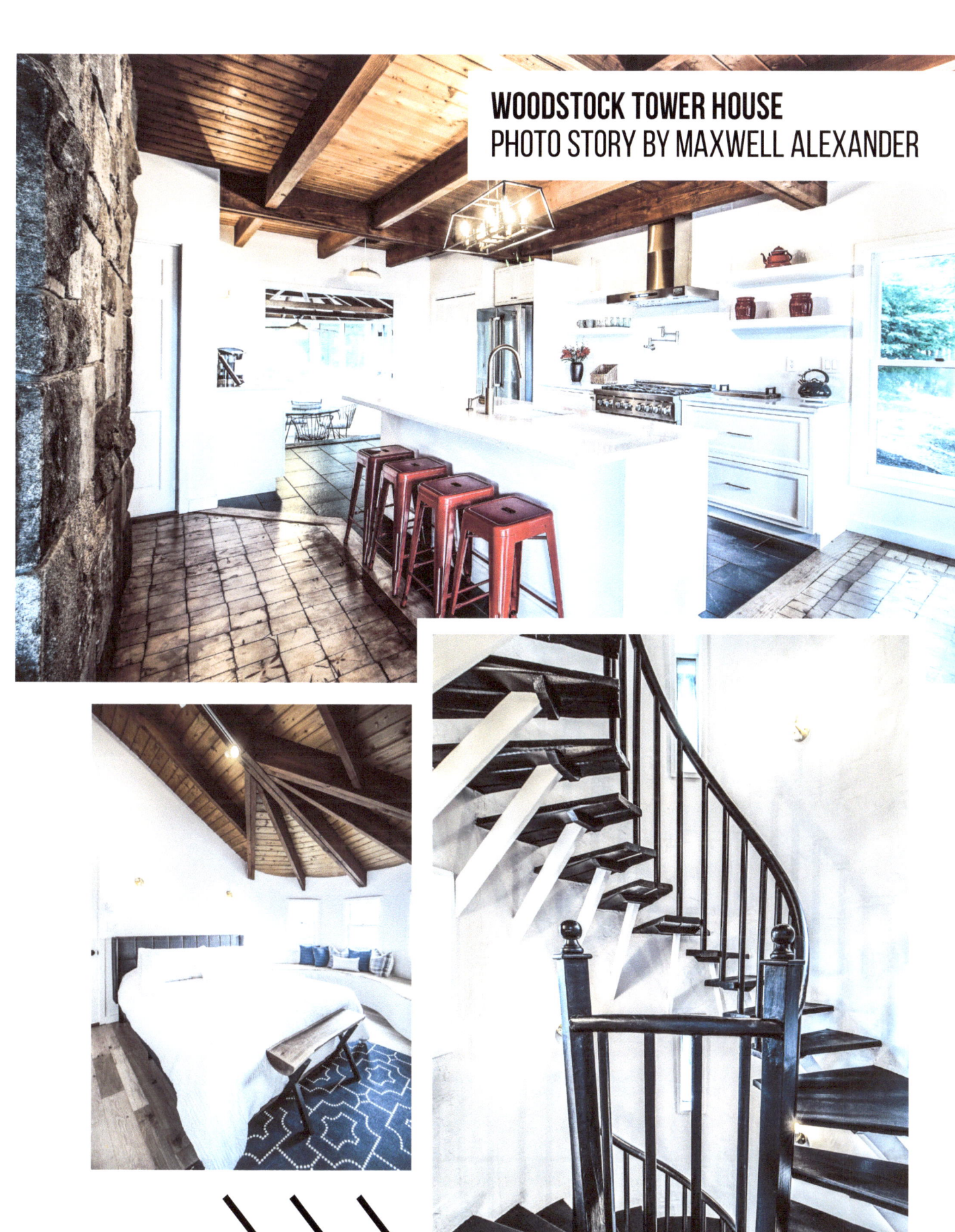

WOODSTOCK TOWER HOUSE
PHOTO STORY BY MAXWELL ALEXANDER

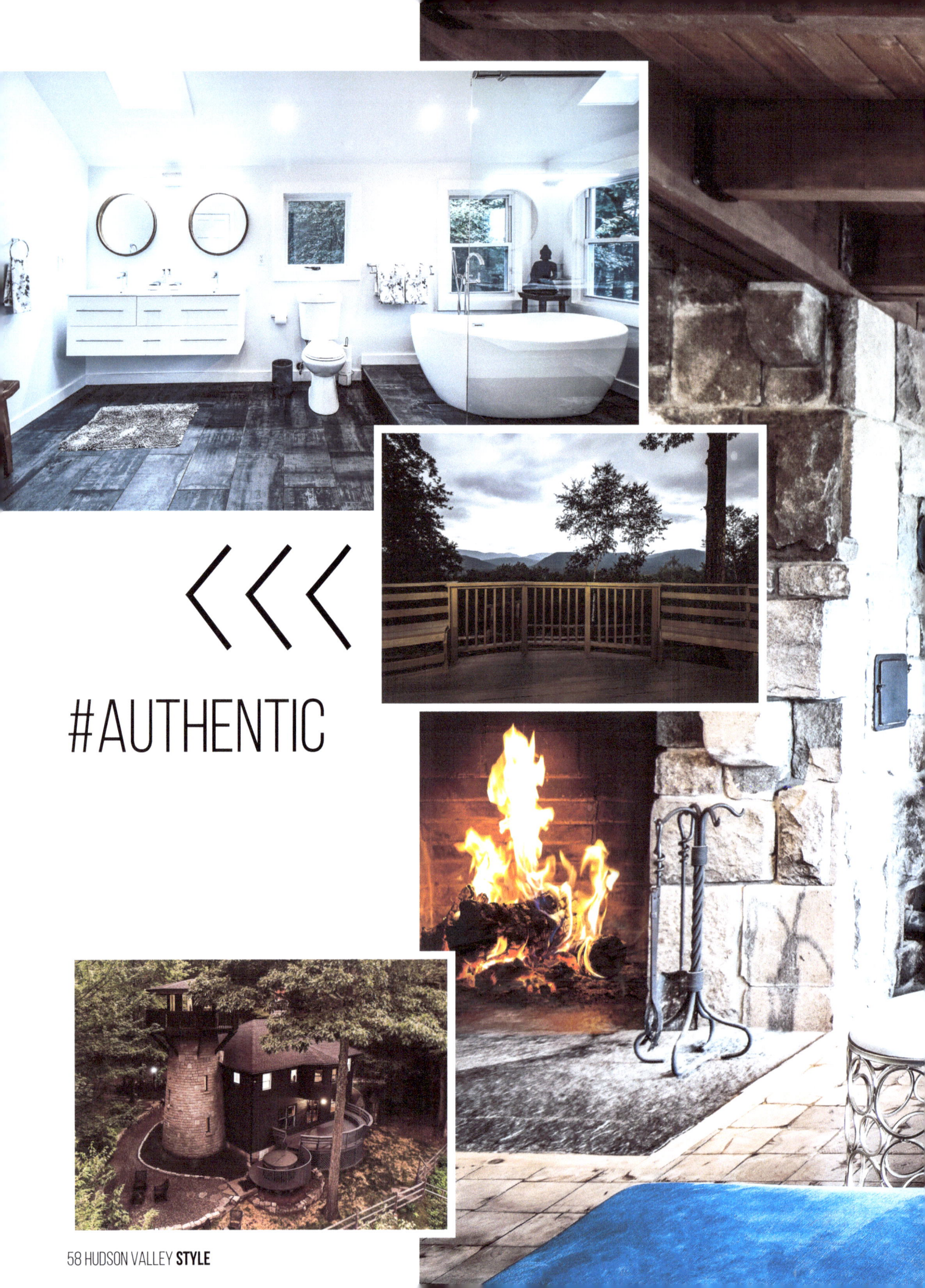

#AUTHENTIC

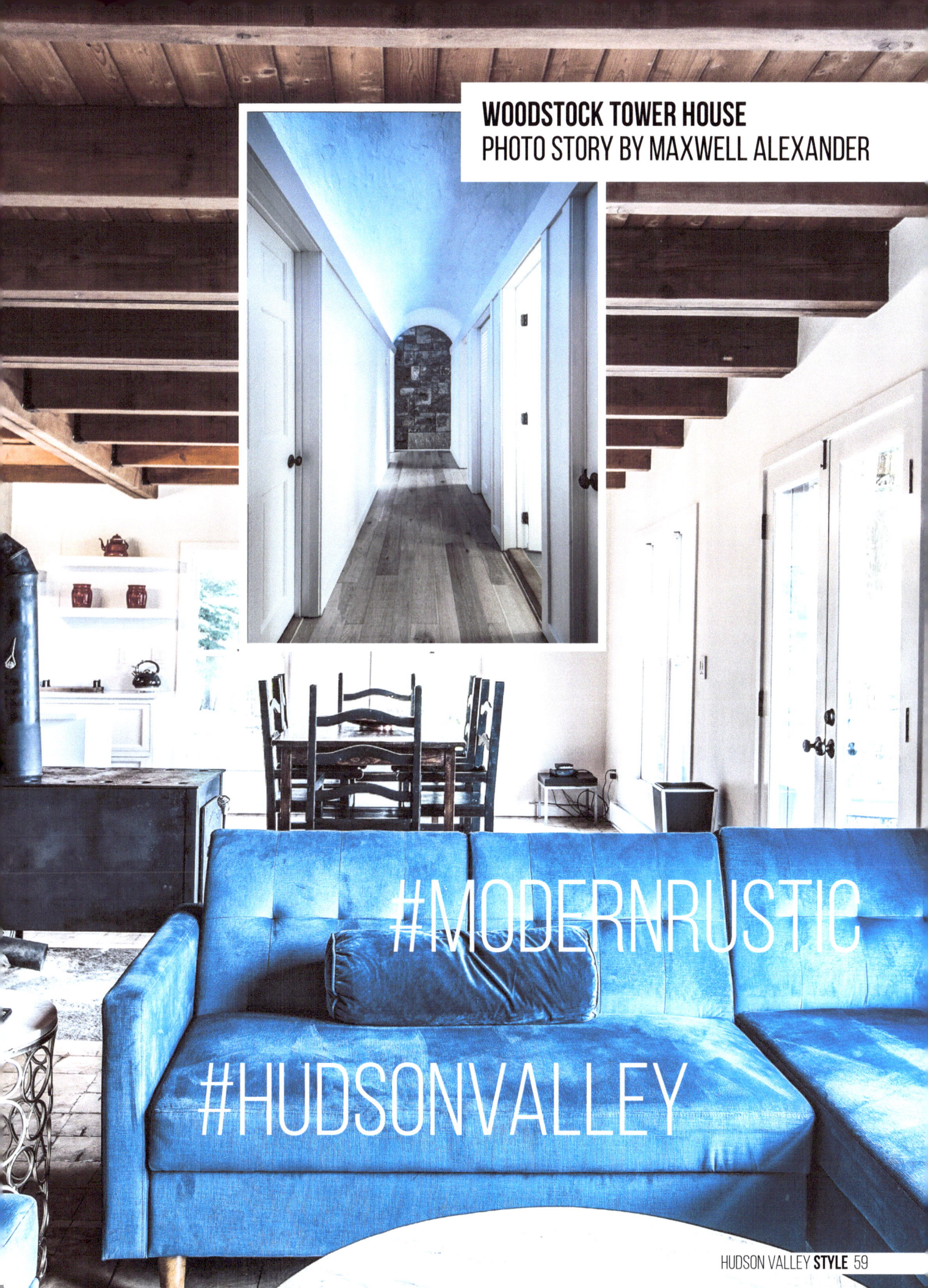

WOODSTOCK TOWER HOUSE
PHOTO STORY BY MAXWELL ALEXANDER

#MODERNRUSTIC

#HUDSONVALLEY

1-YEAR ONLINE BODYBUILDING PROGRAM

DESIGNER ★ ★BODY™

MAXWELL ALEXANDER .FITNESS

TECHNOLOGY-POWERED 24/7 TRAINING
1-Year Online or In-Person Bodybuilding Program

START YOUR JOURNEY TODAY!
Sign up at **MaxwellAlexander.Fitness**

www.ingramcontent.com/pod-product-compliance
Lightning Source LLC
Chambersburg PA
CBHW051210220526
45473CB00003B/977